HA

Co

Th r
uni e
ref l
the f
the .
All s
wil s
of

Brian A. Rutherford is Assistant Secretary of the International Accounting Standards Committee. He qualified as an accountant whilst working in the international headquarters of Bowater Industries and subsequently spent nine years as a lecturer in accounting at the University of Kent at Canterbury. He has published a book on financial reporting in the public sector and more than two dozen articles.

Robert T. Wearing worked as a financial analyst in industry for three years after qualifying as a chartered accountant. He has taught accounting for seven years and is now a lecturer in accounting at the University of Essex. He has published several articles on financial reporting.

CASES IN COMPANY FINANCIAL REPORTING

B. A. RUTHERFORD
BA Ph.D FCCA

Assistant Secretary
International Accounting Standards Committee
and Honorary Research Fellow
University of Kent at Canterbury

R. T. WEARING
BA MSc. FCA

Lecturer
University of Essex

Harper & Row, Publishers
London

Cambridge
Mexico City
New York
Philadelphia

San Francisco
São Paulo
Singapore
Sydney

First published 1987

Harper & Row Ltd
28 Tavistock Street
London WC2E 7PN

British Library Cataloguing in Publication Data
Rutherford, B.A.
Cases in company financial reporting.
1. Corporations——Great Britain——
Accounting——Study and teaching
2. Financial statements——Great Britain——
Case studies
I. Title II. Wearing, R.T.
658. 1'512'0722 HF5686.C7

ISBN 0-06-318371-4

Typeset by Bookworm Typesetting, Manchester
Printed and bound by Redwood Burn Ltd, Trowbridge

To our Parents

Contents

Series Editor's Foreword

One of the original aims of the Accounting Standards Committee was to narrow the areas of difference and variety in UK accounting practice. It was to do this by publishing authoritative statements on best accounting practice with the intention that these statements would be definitive. Since 1970 the Accounting Standards Committee has been very prolific; it has issued more than twenty Statements of Standard Accounting Practice (SSAPs) and more than forty exposure drafts (EDs) and discussion documents. Although many of these publications have dealt with the treatment of particular items in the balance sheet or profit and loss account, for example stocks, research and development and depreciation, some have considered additional accounting reports such as source and application of funds statements and value added statements, and some have attempted to introduce alternative measurement systems, for example current cost accounting.

The Accounting Standards Committee has undoubtedly succeeded in reducing the number of acceptable accounting methods for dealing with particular items, but it has not been able to provide definitive solutions which have been acceptable to all parties. The authors of *Cases in Company Financial Reporting* demonstrate clearly that areas of difference and variety of accounting practice are alive and well in the UK today. Indeed, there is probably as much controversy now surrounding the content and format of published accounts as there was before the Accounting Standards Committee began its programme of work nearly twenty years ago.

Using material from the published financial statements of leading British companies the authors explore the reasons why particular accounting treatments have been selected or why additional non-statutory information has been disclosed voluntarily. In this way the reader has to consider not only the technical accounting issues involved but also the economic and sometimes even the political context in which those decisions were made. Thus, in addition to the financial statements themselves the authors provide background information about the industry, structure and personality of the company. In this way the individual cases are brought to life and provide a very effective means of understanding the complex issues that influence the nature of financial reporting practice in the UK. At the end of each chapter there is a series of questions which can be used to focus discussion on the relevant aspects of the case study and, like accounting standards themselves, there are no definitive solutions.

Cases in Company Financial Reporting is an exciting and innovative book on the subject of financial accounting. It can be used by both professional and degree students in conjunction with a conventional financial accounting textbook or as a stand-alone book, probably for students in their final year of an accounting or business studies degree, who have some previous knowledge of the main concepts and techniques of financial accounting. It is also a very informative book for accountants and managers who are deciding between alternative accounting treatments and who wish to evaluate the various arguments used in favour of each alternative. It is therefore a great pleasure to welcome this book into the Harper & Row Series in Accounting and Finance.

Michael Sherer

Preface

This book contains a variety of case studies in financial reporting, most based on 'real-life' cases, designed to be used in the teaching of financial accounting techniques, accounting policy and the interpretation of financial statements. The volume is intended to supplement an orthodox teaching textbook by providing British case material which can be used to investigate the pragmatic and political dimensions to financial reporting; the technical aspects of the cases under study are not covered in any detail except where topics are not normally dealt with in the standard textbooks. Most of the cases have been designed to illustrate one or more technical problems in financial reporting as well as the scope for pragmatism and the pursuit of 'political' goals which such problems provide.

The use of case study material in the teaching of financial accounting is not yet common, and the Introduction provides some guidance to students on how to set about developing an answer to case study questions. Athough we suggest a variety of questions for each of the cases in the book, teachers may wish to develop alternative questions appropriate to the structure and approach of individual courses.

Since they are designed to augment an orthodox textbook, and to be used flexibly within a course, the cases in the book are suitable for use on any academic or professional course in financial accounting beyond an elementary level.

We are very grateful to those organizations who have given us permission to use material drawn from their financial statements in the cases and to the various regulatory agencies who have allowed us to reproduce extracts from their publications. We are also grateful to our colleagues and students at the Universities of Essex and Kent for all that they have contributed to our understanding – and teaching – of the subject over the years. Deficiencies in the text remain, of course, solely our own responsibility.

B. A. Rutherford, Canterbury; R. T. Wearing, Colcheseter *September 1986*

Acknowledgements

The permission of the following organizations to reproduce material is gratefully acknowledged:

Accounting Standards Committee
Bassett Foods plc
Bemrose Corporation plc
British Airways plc
British Telecommunications plc
H. P. Bulmer Holdings plc
Burmah Oil plc
Council of the Stock Exchange
Imperial Chemical Industries plc
International Accounting Standards Committee
Laporte Industries (Holdings) plc
Marks and Spencer plc
Marshalls Halifax plc
Wm Morrison Supermarkets plc
Pearson plc
Reed International plc
Tarmac plc
Tesco plc
Ultramar plc
Whessoe plc
Woolworth Holdings plc

Certain extracts from financial statements may constitute abridged accounts under the terms of section 255 of the Companies Act 1985 and where this is so full accounts, on which the auditors of the companies concerned have given unqualified reports, have been or will be delivered to the Registrar of Companies.

Introduction: Working on a Case Study

The case studies in this volume are designed to supplement orthodox financial accounting textbooks by offering real contexts and real data for examination. The cases are all British and have been selected to illustrate a wide range of important issues in contemporary financial reporting. Most of the cases cover a specific and well-defined technical 'problem area' such as goodwill or depreciation: however, they also provide an opportunity to investigate the strengths and weaknesses of the accounting process itself. Some of the cases have been selected for use in dealing with more general topics such as ratio analysis. A few are based on events which have played a significant part in the development of accounting standardization, and thus go some way to show why modern financial reporting has evolved in the way it has.

Almost all the cases in the book use real – and identified – companies and real accounts; the few cases employing hypothetical data are based on real contexts. The use of realistic cases means that the questions to be studied are directly related to the world of the practising accountant and should thus be more interesting for the student. However, realism can cause problems as well as create interest; the purpose of this Introduction is to explain how and why some of these problems arise and to suggest how they can be handled for the purposes of working on a case study.

DESIRABLE QUALITIES OF ACCOUNTING INFORMATION

The modern approach to financial reporting holds that accounting information should be *useful*. This means that those who have a legitimate claim to be provided with accounting information should be given what they need, within reasonable limits, to enable them to take the decisions confronting them on a sound basis. In order to be useful, accounting information should be *relevant* to the decision to be taken and *reliable*.

To determine what information will be relevant, it is necessary to discover who uses accounting reports and what decisions they need to take. It is generally considered that the main users of financial reports in Great Britain are shareholders, and that they employ financial information predominantly to take investment decisions, that is to decide whether to buy, hold or sell securities. Shareholders range from private individuals, perhaps owning only a few shares, to major institutions, such as pension funds and insurance companies, which may hold a significant proportion of a company's shares. Institutional investors usually employ specialist financial analysts to interpret the accounts of companies in which they are interested; small investors may also seek specialist advice from, for example, their accountants or stockbrokers.

Investors generally buy shares in order to benefit from future dividends and from increases in the market value of those shares. An enterprise's capacity to pay dividends, and the market's valuation of its shares, are generally related to its own profitability and ability to generate cash; thus, *future* returns for shareholders depend on the *future* profitability of the enterprise. Ideally then, investors require information about future profitability.

Unfortunately, perhaps, no well-understood mechanism exists for generating information about the future, at any rate in the complex and unstable world of commercial activity. Hence, shareholders are provided with information to enable them to form their own view about likely future performance, rather than with the final information they need to take a decision. Much of the information given to shareholders relates to past performance. They can feed this information into their expectations about the organization's future, for example by extrapolating past trends. They may also use the information to decide whether management's performance has been adequate or whether it should be replaced.

Shareholders are not the only group in society who are considered to have legitimate claims on financial information. Amongst other groups are lenders and creditors, employees and customers. The information needs of these groups will vary from case to case, although in general the needs of lenders and other creditors, who are normally concerned about the security of their funds, are most closely related to those of shareholders.

In practice, the complex and uncertain relationship between the decisions to be taken and the data actually available in the real world, together with the competing needs of different groups of users, make it difficult to prescribe in any detail what information should be provided.

If it is to be useful, information must be reliable as well as relevant. Accounting measures are reliable if there is a high degree of correspondence between the numbers or descriptions reported and the underlying phenomena they purport to represent. Information must be reasonably free of error and bias, and must not be drawn up to achieve predetermined outcomes when used in decision-making. As a practical matter, correspondence between accounting numbers and underlying phenomena is not enough: information must be verifiable, that is to say it must be possible to demonstrate the degree of correspondence by means, for example, of an audit.

CHARACTERISTICS OF REAL ACCOUNTING INFORMATION

In the real world, accounting information is always imperfect and incomplete. This is so for a variety of reasons.

1. As explained above, there are many difficulties in specifying what information will be relevant in any particular context.
2. The phenomena which financial reports purport to measure are complex and ill-understood, so that testing for faithful representation is itself problematic.
3. There will often be a need to trade off one desirable quality for another so that, for example, highly relevant information (such as specific indications of the directors' expectations about the future) is omitted from reports because of difficulties in verifying it.
4. The preparation of accounting information has a cost – as does its subsequent processing by users – so that it is desirable to limit the production of information to the level at which benefits exceed cost. Unfortunately, it is usually very difficult to determine what benefits are derived from any particular piece of information so that the application of a cost-benefit test adds to the complexity of deciding what information should be published.
5. Many of the uses to which accounting information is put require comparisons to be made between the same company's performance through time, or between the performance of different companies. As innovations in financial reporting are introduced, comparison is made more difficult as information is produced on a new basis which may not be consistent with that used previously or by other enterprises.
6. Management may not wish to publish information for fear that it may prove useful to competitors or other outside parties.
7. Management may have its own motives for not wishing to publish a piece of information – for example, its own performance may be shown in a poor light.

Even when there appears to be no reason for refusing to disclose a piece of information, management is often reluctant to do so, perhaps feeling it may be committed to continuing with the disclosure in subsequent years – when it might prefer not to – or to further disclosures which it would not wish to make. In general, directors have proved reluctant over the years to disclose much beyond what they are required to by law and other regulations.

WORKING ON A CASE STUDY

Because the case studies in this volume reflect the real world the issues they raise are complex and strongly interrelated. Problems rarely come 'one at a time' and are not usually capable of perfect resolution. Solving one problem may create others. For example, in 1977 SSAP 12 was published dealing with the issue of accounting for depreciation. However, investment companies objected that it was not appropriate to depreciate properties held as an investment. As a result such assets were treated as a special case, and in 1981 an additional standard, SSAP 19, was issued dealing specifically with investment properties. The 1981 standard put forward the view that it is more important to report changes in the current value of investment properties than to provide for depreciation.

For the reasons discussed in the previous section, the available information will be imperfect and incomplete. This is what provides the challenge and the stimulation of working on a realistic case study: a complete, 'tidy' solution to the problem is not expected; what is needed is the best response to the 'untidiness' of the real world that is possible under the circumstances.

In working on a case study, it is worth bearing the following points in mind.

1. Although they have been edited down from the originals, the documents provided for each case give a mass of information, not all of which will necessarily be relevant to the questions raised. Further, the documents are not structured so as to provide information in the order needed to respond to the questions, or in any particular order of importance. This is just one aspect of the realism of the cases! As a result it is a good idea to read all the documents through rapidly once before proceeding to work on the case, to get an idea of the information they contain and how it is presented.
2. Having read the documents, it is important to try to understand the context of the case. To which organization does the case relate? Who owns it? What other parties have a major interest in it? What does it do? Is it successful? What major events have occurred – or are likely to occur – affecting the organization and the parties interested in it? What other aspects of the situation are likely to affect the organization's future? For instance, changes taking place in the national economy may influence readers' perceptions about the desirability or usefulness of some accounting treatments. A specific example of this would be recent changes to the corporation tax system which are likely to affect readers' views on the need to provide for deferred taxation. Changes in the rate of inflation will be likely to affect perceptions about the importance of using a basis of accounting which reflects changes in prices.
3. It is also important to understand the information flows in the case. Who are the users of the information? Are they shareholders, employees, creditors or government? What information are they receiving? For what decisions are they likely to want to use the information?
4. Questions will usually bear on both the relevance and the reliability of information. To specify what information will be relevant to users it is necessary to show how they will use it in taking decisions. As already indicated, the relationships to be examined here will be both complex and uncertain.
5. To investigate the reliability of information it is necessary to specify the

underlying phenomena which are being represented. Do the accounting numbers reported correspond reasonably closely to the phenomena they purport to represent, without excessive bias or error, and are they verifiable?

6. Strategies for dealing with the 'information gaps' which arise when data is incomplete or imperfect include:

   (a) Find some means of approximating the missing information, for example by extrapolating a past trend or making an inference from information that is available. For example, shareholders wishing to hide their identity can use nominees to hold the shares on their behalf. This makes it difficult to establish what proportion of shares are held by any shareholder group (for example, pension funds). It may be possible, however, to use previous research into the distribution of such shareholdings to estimate the ownership pattern of any particular company.
   (b) Adopt an alternative approach which does not require the missing information. For example, one might take the view that return on capital employed (operating profit divided by net assets) is a useful indicator of company performance. If there has been a marked change in net assets during the period in question, there are good arguments for using an average figure based on opening and closing net assets in the calculation of return on capital. However, if a comparative figure for the return in the previous period is needed, this can only be calculated if the opening net asset figure for the previous period is available. If data for only two periods is available, an alternative, 'second-best' solution is to base the calculation on closing net assets. This might produce less reliable data year by year but, by allowing a trend to be calculated, yield a more informative overall picture.
   (c) Answer as much of the question as possible and specify what additional information would be needed to complete the answer.

Many of the questions ask what information should be included in an enterprise's financial statements or how such information should be measured: as indicated above, the most crucial factors to be considered in responding to such questions are *relevance* and *reliability*.

Case 1
Research and Development Expenditure: Rolls-Royce

OBJECTIVES

1. To investigate the nature of an *asset*.
2. To examine the problems that can arise in the absence of an agreed set of fundamental definitions.
3. To explore problems of assigning transactions to categories.
4. To consider the impact of uncertainty on financial reporting.
5. To discuss the role of economic interests and political lobbying in the standard-setting process.

MATERIALS

1. Selected definitions of an asset (Exhibit 1.1).
2. Extracts from the annual report and accounts of Rolls-Royce Ltd for the year ended 31 December 1969:

   (a) consolidated profit and loss account (Exhibit 1.2);
   (b) consolidated balance sheet (Exhibit 1.3);
   (c) notes 3, 7 and 13 (Exhibit 1.4);
   (d) paragraph 3 of the report of the directors (Exhibit 1.5);
   (e) auditors' report (Exhibit 1.6);

3. Extracts from ED 14 (issued January 1975) (Exhibit 1.7).

4. Extracts from ED 17 (issued April 1976) (Exhibit 1.8).
5. Extracts from SSAP 13 (issued December 1977) (Exhibit 1.9).
6. Extracts from submissions on ED 14 (Exhibit 1.10).

INTRODUCTION

Rolls-Royce's balance sheet at 31 December 1968 included £12.2 million of research and development expenditure carried forward to be amortized against future revenues earned from exploiting that research and development activity. In the following year a further £5.3 million was capitalized whilst only £1.2 million was amortized; after adjusting for tax effects, the amount of expenditure to be carried forward should have risen to £14.5 million; in fact only £3.5 million appeared on the balance sheet. This was because the directors 'consider[ed] it prudent to make a special provision . . . against the risk of non-recovery of total development costs' (note 7). The write-down required was more than double the company's profit after taxation. The case focused attention sharply on the dangers of capitalizing costs where their recovery is uncertain and undoubtedly influenced the accounting profession's attitude to research and development expenditure in the following years.

The ASC's first exposure draft dealing with research and development expenditure was ED 14, published in January 1975. Extracts from ED 14 are given in Exhibit 1.7. The draft received a substantial measure of approval from all quarters. However, four companies responding to the ASC's invitation to comment on the draft opposed the requirement to write off all development expenditure. Three of these were in the aerospace industry, and their trade association made a submission in similar terms. The extract from the submission of Westland is typical. The minority of professional firms who opposed immediate write-off used technical arguments, rather than concerning themselves with the impact of the requirement on the cash flows of commercial enterprises. An extract from Whinney Murray's submission is given in Exhibit 1.10.

The ASC responded to the submissions they received by publishing a revised draft, ED 17, in April 1976. Following further submissions, SSAP 13 was adopted in December 1977. Extracts from the two documents are given in Exhibits 1.8 and 1.9.

ANALYSIS

When expenditure is incurred, the framework of double entry bookkeeping requires the creation of a debit balance. At the end of the period the issue which arises is quite straightforward in bookkeeping terms. Should the debit balance be charged in the profit and loss account as an expense of the period or be carried forward in the balance sheet as an asset? The issue is normally addressed from the direction of the balance sheet: has an asset been created and does it still exist? The response to this question will clearly depend on the meaning of the term 'asset'. Unfortunately there is no universal agreement on what accountants mean when they employ the term. A select list of definitions is given in Exhibit 1.1; a search of the textbooks on any library shelf will reveal more.

Expenditure on research and development highlights one important feature of many debit balances: it is rarely possible to be completely certain that they will yield any future benefit for the organization, simply because they, like the accountants who record them, exist in an uncertain world. In the face of uncertainty, two of the four 'fundamental accounting concepts' discussed in SSAP 1 appear to conflict. The accruals concept requires that expenditure be carried forward so that it can be matched with the revenue it will generate, whilst prudence argues for an immediate write-off.

A second issue which arises is whether expenditure on research and development should be separately *disclosed*, regardless of how it is treated in the financial statements. In order to require disclosure, it is, of course, necessary to define what outlays fall within the scope of research and development.

QUESTIONS

1. Compare and contrast the various definitions of an asset given in Exhibit 1.1, adding any others you can find. Indicate which you prefer and why.
2. Was it reasonable to regard Rolls-Royce's research and development expenditure as an asset (according to your definition) at 31 December 1968? Do not use the information available from the 1969 accounts in arriving at your view.
3. Would you, as an analyst, have been satisfied with the level of disclosure relating to the write-off in the 1969 accounts?
4. Analyse the changes between ED 14, ED 17 and SSAP 13, paying particular attention to the distinction between *treatment* and *disclosure* and to whether provisions are *mandatory* or *permissive*.
5. 'Since expenditure on research and development will generally be level through time, immediate expensing and capitalization will yield the same result: it is thus of little consequence which treatment is adopted.' Do you consider that this argument is valid?
6. Do you consider that the argument for writing off research and development expenditure immediately is one of 'convenience and expediency' (Whinney Murray)?
7. 'This country spends far too little on research and development as it is. Any accounting requirement which discourages companies from undertaking research – such as a rule that what they spend must be charged against profit immediately, no matter how promising the line of research is in terms of future profits – will have dangerous consequences for the economy and must be resisted.' Comment.
8. To what extent were the changes between ED 14 and SSAP 13 a result of 'political' pressure? Was this a bad thing? Why did professional firms use

'technical' arguments against ED 14 when commercial enterprises argued in terms of economic consequences?

9. If you were capitalizing development costs, how would you treat:

   (a) the cost of renting a laboratory used to carry out work on a project?
   (b) general overheads (such as heating and lighting) of the research and development department?
   (c) the cost of a market survey to test the commercial viability of a product in the course of development?

FURTHER READING

Hope, T. and Gray, R. (1982) Power and policy making: the development of an R & D standard, *Journal of Business Finance and Accounting*, pp. 531-58.

EXHIBIT 1.1 SELECTED DEFINITIONS OF AN ASSET

Accounting Principles Board

Economic resources of an enterprise that are recognized and measured in conformity with generally accepted accounting principles. Assets also include certain deferred charges that are not resources but that are recognized and measured in conformity with generally accepted accounting principles.

(Accounting Principles Board (1970) Statement No. 4, American Institute of Certified Public Accountants.)

Bird

Items of value owned by the organization.

(Bird, P. A. (1983) *Understanding Company Accounts* (2nd ed), Pitman, London.)

Financial Accounting Standards Board

Assets are probable future economic benefits obtained or controlled by a particular entity as a result of past transactions or events.

(Financial Accounting Standards Board (1985) Statement of Financial Accounting Concepts No. 6.)

Parker

Any property, tangible or intangible, from which future benefits are expected, and of which a company has a legal right of use as a result of a past or present transaction.

(Parker, R. H. (1982) *Understanding Company Financial Statements* (2nd ed), Penguin, Harmondsworth, Middlesex.)

Sprouse and Moonitz

Expected future economic benefits, rights to which have been acquired by the enterprise as a result of some current or past transaction.

(Sprouse, R. J. and Moonitz, M. (1962) *A Tentative Set of Broad Accounting Principles for Business Enterprises*, Accounting Research Study No. 3, American Institute of Certified Public Accountants.)

EXHIBIT 1.2 ROLLS-ROYCE LTD: CONSOLIDATED PROFIT AND LOSS ACCOUNT

CONSOLIDATED PROFIT AND LOSS ACCOUNT FOR THE YEAR ENDED 31st DECEMBER 1969

THE PROFIT HAS BEEN EARNED AS FOLLOWS

		1969	1968
		£000	£000
Revenue from all sources	Note 1	301,436	321,726
Costs of manufacture, selling and administration	Note 2	276,035	291,308
		25,401	30,418
Research and development	Note 3	10,286	6,364
		15,115	24,054
Interest charges	Note 4	8,708	8,135
Profit before taxation		6,407	15,919
Taxation	Note 5	2,064	6,962
		4,343	8,957
Profit attributable to outside shareholders of subsidiary companies		118	75
Profit for the year after taxation	Note 6	4,225	8,882

APPROPRIATION ACCOUNT

		1969	1968
Profit for the year after taxation		4,225	8,882
Transfer from (to) profits retained in the business		10,748	(1,506)
		14,973	7,376
Special provision of £20,000,000 less anticipated tax relief	Note 7	11,000	—
Dividends paid and proposed: Interim of 3% (1968: 4%)		1,988	2,263
Final of 3% (1968: 7.784%)		1,985	5,154
		14,973	7,417
less: income tax retained		—	41
		14,973	7,376

Notes on and forming part of the consolidated profit and loss account are given on pages 10 to 12 inclusive.

EXHIBIT 1.3 ROLLS-ROYCE LTD: CONSOLIDATED BALANCE SHEET

CONSOLIDATED BALANCE SHEET AT 31st DECEMBER 1969

ASSETS LESS CURRENT LIABILITIES		1969	1968
CURRENT ASSETS:		£000	£000
Cash and bank balances		848	1,118
Debtors	Note 8	110,947	118,026
Stocks	Note 9	112,101	115,642
		223,896	**234,786**
CURRENT LIABILITIES:			
Bank indebtedness	Note 10	37,027	32,375
Acceptances		17,000	14,000
Creditors		62,305	63,579
Taxation		1,864	6,851
Proposed final dividend		1,985	5,154
		120,181	**121,959**
NET CURRENT ASSETS		**103,715**	**112,827**
INVESTMENTS – unquoted	Note 11	6,892	7,675
PROPERTY AND PLANT	Note 12	82,482	69,819
RESEARCH AND DEVELOPMENT	Note 13	3,451	12,179
GOODWILL, PATENTS AND TRADE MARKS at cost less amount written off		24,709	24,709
		221,249	**227,209**

FINANCED AS FOLLOWS			
CAPITAL AND RESERVES:			
Share capital	Note 14	66,325	66,264
Capital reserves	Note 15	57,241	53,050
Profits retained in the business	Note 16	20,213	30,967
		143,779	**150,281**
DEBENTURE AND LOAN STOCK	Note 17	56,650	57,163
DEFERRED LIABILITIES	Note 18	20,203	19,225
INTERESTS OF OUTSIDE SHAREHOLDERS OF SUBSIDIARY COMPANIES		617	540
		221,249	**227,209**

On behalf of the Board — DENNING PEARSON, WHITNEY W. STRAIGHT, **Directors**

Notes on and forming part of the balance sheet are given on pages 13 to 17 inclusive.

EXHIBIT 1.4 ROLLS-ROYCE LTD: EXTRACTS FROM NOTES ON ACCOUNTS

Notes on Consolidated Profit and Loss Account

3 RESEARCH AND DEVELOPMENT

	RB211-22	Other Products	1969 Total	1968 Total
	£000	£000	£000	£000
Net expenditure during year	5,342	9,076	14,418	14,082
Change in amount to be carried forward as research and development asset (See note 13)	5,342	(1,210)	4,132	7,718
Charge to profit and loss account	—	10,286	**10,286**	**6,364**

7 SPECIAL PROVISION FOR RESEARCH AND DEVELOPMENT ON RB 211-22

It has been the company's practice since the inception of the RB 211-22 programme in 1967 to carry forward the net development expenditure, after deducting Government participation and investment grants on prototypes, for amortisation against future sales. In 1969, following this policy, net expenditure of £5,342,000 was added to the research and development asset.

As stated in paragraph 3 of the Directors' Report, there must inevitably be uncertainties as to the ultimate recovery of research and development costs of this engine. Accordingly the directors consider it prudent to make a special provision of £20,000,000 against the risk of non-recovery of total development costs.

Taxation relief on the special provision has been anticipated because there is sufficient in the tax equalisation account at 31st December 1969 to ensure relief is obtainable.

EXHIBIT 1.4 CONTINUED

Notes on Balance Sheets

13 **RESEARCH AND DEVELOPMENT**

RB 211-22

Net development expenditure after deducting Government participation and investment grants on prototypes is carried forward for amortisation against future sales. (See note 7).

ENGINES CURRENTLY IN PRODUCTION

An assessment has been made of the research and development recoverable from future sales of engines on order at 31st December 1969, and from the sale of spares still to be delivered for engines in service and on order. After deducting amounts repayable to H M Government in consideration for their participation in development costs from such sales, and estimated continuing development expenditure for the next three years, the balance is carried forward.

In both cases a deduction of 45% for tax equalisation is made in arriving at the value to be placed on the research and development asset in the balance sheet.

		1969	1968
RB 211-22	£000	£000	£000
Gross expenditure to date		48,222	16,307
less: Government participation in research and development	31,199		
Estimated investment grants on prototypes	6,070	37,269	10,696
Amount carried forward (before tax equalisation)		10,953	5,611
ENGINES CURRENTLY IN PRODUCTION			
Development to be recovered at 31st December 1968	16,535		13,896
Reduction (increase) in amount carried forward at 31st December 1969 (See note 3)	1,210		(2,639)
Amount carried forward (before tax equalisation)		15,325	16,535
		26,278	22,146
less: tax equalisation		11,827	9,967
		14,451	12,179
less: special provision net of tax (See note 7)		11,000	—
		3,451	**12,179**

The agreed Government participation to the launching costs of the RB 211-22 is £47,100,000 of which £39,400,000 relates to development costs. Of the total £31,731,000 had been received by 31st December 1969.

EXHIBIT 1.5 ROLLS-ROYCE LTD: EXTRACT FROM DIRECTORS' REPORT

Report of the Directors

RB 211-22 Engine

Today's estimates of sales and costs of the RB 211-22 project would achieve full recovery of total estimated research and development expenditure.

However, consideration of a long range project such as the RB 211-22 engine involves estimates of both sales and costs relating to many years in the future and the recovery of the total RB 211-22 research and development expenditure is dependent on the actual costs and ultimate sales of the engine.

In addition, development of this advanced engine and the application of carbon fibre materials is proving to be more expensive than anticipated when the programme was launched. Furthermore, the rates of escalation of labour, material and other costs already experienced and now estimated up to full scale production of the engine are substantially higher than could reasonably have been expected and will add materially to the total expenditure.

In view of these uncertainties the directors consider it prudent to make a special provision of £20,000,000 against the risk of non-recovery of total development costs.

Your directors are conscious that the final outcome of the RB 211-22 project may significantly affect the financial position of the company.

EXHIBIT 1.6 ROLLS-ROYCE LTD: AUDITORS' REPORT

Auditors' Report to the Members of Rolls-Royce Limited

In our opinion, based on our examination and on the reports of other firms who have audited the accounts of certain subsidiaries, the accounts and notes set out on pages 8 to 19 comply with the Companies Acts 1948 and 1967 and, read in the context of the contingencies and the provision of £20,000,000 mentioned in paragraph 3 of the Directors' Report, give, so far as concerns members of the company, a true and fair view of the state of affairs at 31st December 1969 of the company and of the group and of the profit of the group for the year ended on that date.

TOUCHE ROSS & CO.
Chartered Accountants

3 London Wall Buildings
London EC2

22nd June 1970

EXHIBIT 1.7 ED 14: ACCOUNTING FOR RESEARCH AND DEVELOPMENT

Part 1 – Explanatory note

Basic concepts

The accounting policies to be followed in respect of research and development expenditure must have regard to the fundamental accounting concepts, including the accruals concept by which revenue and costs are accrued, matched and dealt with in the period to which they relate and the 'prudence' concept by which revenue and profits are not anticipated but are recognized only when realized in the form either of cash or of other assets the ultimate cash realization of which can be established with reasonable certainty. It is a corollary of the prudence concept that expenditure should be written off in the period in which it arises unless its relationship to the revenue of a future period can be established with reasonable certainty.

The different types of research and development expenditure

2. The term 'research and development' is currently used to cover a wide range of activities. Classification of the related expenditure is often dependent on the type of business and its organization. However, it is generally possible to recognize three broad categories of activity, namely, pure research (work directed primarily towards the advancement of knowledge), applied research (work directed primarily towards exploiting pure research, other than work defined as development expenditure) and development (work directed towards the introduction or improvement of specific products or processes).
3. The definitions of the different types of research and development used in this statement have been based on those used by the Organization for Economic Co-operation and Development which are used on a worldwide basis for the purposes of collecting data on this subject.
4. The dividing line between these categories of expenditure will often be indistinct and particular expenditure may have characteristics of more than one category. This is particularly apparent when new products are developed through research and development to production, when the activities may have characteristics of both development and production.

The accounting treatment of research and development

5. Expenditure incurred on pure and applied research can be regarded as part of a continuing operation required to maintain a company's business and its competitive position. In general, one particular period rather than another will not be expected to benefit and therefore it is appropriate that these costs

EXHIBIT 1.7 CONTINUED

should be written off as they are incurred.

6. The development of new and improved products is, however, distinguishable from pure and applied research. Expenditure on such development is normally undertaken with a reasonable expectation of specific commercial success and of future benefits arising from the work, either from increased revenue and related profits or from reduced costs. On these grounds it may be argued that such expenditure should be deferred to be matched against the future revenue.
7. It will only be practicable to evaluate the potential future benefits of development expenditure if:

   (a) there is a clearly defined project; and
   (b) the related expenditure is separately identifiable.

8. The outcome of such a project would then need to be examined for:

   (a) its technical feasibility; and
   (b) its ultimate commercial viability considered in the light of factors such as:

      (i) likely market conditions (including competing products);
      (ii) public opinion;
      (iii) consumer and environmental legislation.

9. Furthermore a project will only be of value:

   (a) if further development costs to be incurred on the same project together with related production, selling and administration costs will be more than covered by related future revenues; and
   (b) adequate resources exist, or are reasonably expected to be available, to enable the project to be completed and to provide any consequential increases in working capital.

10. The elements of uncertainty inherent in the considerations set out in paragraphs 8 and 9 are considerable. There will be a need for different persons having differing levels of judgement to be involved in assessing the technical, commercial and financial viability of the project. Combinations of the possible different assessments which they might validly make could produce widely differing assessments of the existence and amounts of future benefits.
11. If these uncertainties are viewed in the context of the concept of prudence, few development projects would be likely to be judged to have sufficient certainty of producing future benefits to justify carrying them forward. While it cannot be denied that there is a theoretical case for carrying forward development expenditure in these few cases, it is nevertheless considered that the combination of rarity of occurrence and considerable

EXHIBIT 1.7 CONTINUED

uncertainties make such a case an insecure foundation for a practical standard. Accordingly, it is proposed to regard as standard accounting practice that research and development expenditure should be written off in the year in which it is incurred, subject to the exceptions noted in paragraph 13.

12. Fixed assets may be acquired or constructed in order to provide facilities for research and/or development activities. The use of such fixed assets will usually extend over a number of accounting periods and accordingly they should be capitalized and written off over their useful life. The depreciation so written off should be included as part of the expenditure on research and development.

Exceptions

13. Where companies enter into a firm contract:

    (a) to carry out development work on behalf of third parties on such terms that the related expenditure is to be fully reimbursed; or
    (b) to develop and manufacture at an agreed price which has been calculated to reimburse the element of development as well as the manufacture.

    such expenditure is akin to work in progress and it would be appropriate to include it under that heading.

14. It should be noted that expenditure incurred in locating and exploiting mineral deposits in the extractive industries does not fall within the definition of research and development used in this accounting standard.

Market research

15. The definitions of research and development expenditure, based on those used by the Organization for Economic Co-operation and Development, do not encompass expenditure on market research. Nevertheless the accounting treatment for expenditure on market research could generally be expected to follow that for research and development expenditure, and thus it would generally be appropriate to write off such expenditure as incurred. Such amounts written off would not fall to be included in the amount to be disclosed as research and development.

EXHIBIT 1.7 CONTINUED

Disclosure

16. The practical standpoint adopted in paragraph *11* above that expenditure on research and development should be written off as incurred is based on the existence of considerable uncertainties and the concept of prudence. It is arguable that a full understanding of the possible effect of such uncertainties upon the state of affairs and profit or loss of a company might indicate disclosure for example of the nature, status and costs of individual research and development projects. It is, however, concluded that to call for such detailed disclosure would be unreasonable. Accordingly it is proposed that disclosure should not be required beyond the total amounts expended.

Part 2 – Definition of terms

Research and development expenditure

17. For the purpose of this statement research and development expenditure means expenditure falling into one or more of the following broad categories (except to the extent that it relates to the extractive industries or is reimbursable by third parties either directly or under the terms of a firm contract to develop and manufacture at a price which has been calculated to reimburse both elements of expenditure):
    - (a) Pure (or basic) research: original investigation undertaken in order to gain new scientific or technical knowledge and understanding. Basic research is not primarily directed towards any specific practical aim or application.
    - (b) Applied research: original investigation undertaken in order to gain new scientific or technical knowledge and directed towards a specific practical aim or objective.
    - (c) Development: the use of scientific or technical knowledge in order to produce new or substantially improved materials, devices, products, processes, systems or services.

Part 3 – Proposed standard accounting practice

Accounting treatment

18. Expenditure on research and development should be written off in the year of expenditure. The cost of fixed assets acquired or constructed in order to provide facilities for research and development activities over a number of

EXHIBIT 1.7 CONTINUED

accounting periods should be capitalized and written off over their useful life.

Disclosure

19. There should be separately disclosed in financial statements the amount expended during the year on research and development. On the first introduction of this standard there should also be disclosed the amount written off in respect of balances of deferred expenditure brought forward. (This will fall to be treated as a prior year adjustment being a consequence of a change in accounting policies.)

EXHIBIT 1.8 ED 17: ACCOUNTING FOR RESEARCH AND DEVELOPMENT (REVISED)

Preface

In January 1975 the Accounting Standards Steering Committee published ED 14, 'Accounting for research and development'. A total of sixty-two replies was received and these have been studied in detail. The view set out in that paper that expenditure on pure and applied research should be written off as incurred received general support.

The conclusion in respect of development expenditure was set out in paragraphs 10 and 11 of ED 14 as follows:

10. The elements of uncertainty inherent in the considerations set out in paragraphs 8 and 9 are considerable. There will be a need for different persons having differing levels of judgement to be involved in assessing the technical, commercial and financial viability of the project. Combinations of the possible different assessments which they might validly make could produce widely differing assessments of the existence and amounts of future benefits.
11. If these uncertainties are viewed in the context of the concept of prudence, few development projects would be likely to be judged to have sufficient certainty of producing future benefits to justify carrying them forward. While it cannot be denied that there is a theoretical case for carrying forward development expenditure in these few cases, it is nevertheless considered that the combination of rarity of occurrence and considerable uncertainties make such a case an insecure foundation for a practical standard. Accordingly, it is proposed to regard as standard accounting practice that research and development expenditure should be written off in the year in which it is incurred, subject to the exceptions noted in paragraph 13.

Paragraph 11 pointed out that a logical case could be made for carrying forward development expenditure in cases where the criteria set out in paragraphs 7, 8 and 9 were met. It was concluded, however, that since the number of such development projects would be small, it would make for uniformity and reduce subjective judgement if such development expenditure were written off in the year in which it is incurred.

A considerable body of opinion has emerged during the exposure period to the effect that in certain industries (particularly aerospace and electronics) many projects are in hand at any one time in respect of which the theoretical case (referred to in paragraph 11 of ED 14) for carrying the expenditure forward could be evidenced. In these circumstances, the Accounting Standards Committee is persuaded that a standard accounting practice which requires all development expenditure to be written off as incurred would be too rigid. A further period of two months has been fixed for consideration of the revised exposure draft.

EXHIBIT 1.8 CONTINUED

Part 1 – Explanatory note

Basic concepts

1. The accounting policies to be followed in respect of research and development expenditure must have regard to the fundamental accounting concepts including the 'accruals' concept by which revenue and costs are accrued, matched and dealt with in the period to which they relate and the 'prudence' concept by which revenue and profits are not anticipated but are recognized only when realized in the form either of cash or of other assets, the ultimate cash realization of which can be established with reasonable certainty. It is a corollary of the prudence concept that expenditure should be written off in the period in which it arises unless its relationship to the revenue of a future period can be established with reasonable certainty.

The different types of research and development expenditure

2. The term 'research and development' is currently used to cover a wide range of activities. Classification of the related expenditure is often dependent on the type of business and its organization. However, it is generally possible to recognize three broad categories of activity, namely, pure research (work directed primarily towards the advancement of knowledge), applied research (work directed primarily towards exploiting pure research other than work defined as development expenditure), and development (work directed towards the introduction or improvement of specific products or processes).
3. The definitions of the different types of research and development used in this statement have been based on those used by the Organization for Economic Co-operation and Development which are used on a worldwide basis for the purposes of collecting data on this subject.
4. The dividing line between these categories of expenditure will often be indistinct and particular expenditure may have characteristics of more than one category. This is particularly apparent when new products are developed through research and development to production, when the activities may have characteristics of both development and production.

The accounting treatment of research and development

5. Expenditure incurred on pure and applied research can be regarded as part of a continuing operation required to maintain a company's business and its competitive position. In general, one particular period rather than another will not be expected to benefit and therefore it is appropriate that these costs should be written off as they are incurred.

EXHIBIT 1.8 CONTINUED

6. The development of new and improved products is, however, distinguishable from pure and applied research. Expenditure on such development is normally undertaken with a reasonable expectation of specific commercial success and of future benefits arising from the work, either from increased revenue and related profits or from reduced costs. On these grounds it may be argued that such expenditure should be deferred to be matched against the future revenue.
7. It will only be practicable to evaluate the potential future benefits of development expenditure if:

   (a) there is a clearly defined project; and
   (b) the related expenditure is separately identifiable.

8. The outcome of such a project would then need to be examined for:

   (a) its technical feasibility; and
   (b) its ultimate commercial viability considered in the light of factors such as:

      (i) likely market conditions (including competing products);
      (ii) public opinion;
      (iii) consumer and environmental legislation.

9. Furthermore a project will only be of value:

   (a) if further development costs to be incurred on the same project together with related production, selling and administration costs will be more than covered by related future revenues; and
   (b) adequate resources exist, or are reasonably expected to be available, to enable the project to be completed and to provide any consequential increases in working capital.

10. The elements of uncertainty inherent in the considerations set out in paragraphs 8 and 9 are considerable. There will be a need for different persons having differing levels of judgement to be involved in assessing the technical, commercial and financial viability of the project. Combinations of the possible different assessments which they might validly make can produce widely differing assessments of the existence and amounts of future benefits.
11. If these uncertainties are viewed in the context of the concept of prudence, the future benefits of most development projects would be too uncertain to justify carrying the expenditure forward. Nevertheless, in certain industries it is considered that there are numbers of major development projects that satisfy the stringent criteria set out in paragraphs 7–9. Accordingly, where expenditure on development projects is judged on a prudent view of

EXHIBIT 1.8 CONTINUED

available evidence to satisfy these criteria, it should be carried forward and amortized over the period expected to benefit.

12. At each accounting date the unamortized balance of development expenditure should be examined project by project to ensure that it still fulfils the criteria in paragraphs 7–9. Where any doubt exists as to the continuation of those circumstances the balance should be written off.
13. Fixed assets may be acquired or constructed in order to provide facilities for research and/or development activities. The use of such fixed assets will usually extend over a number of accounting periods and accordingly they should be capitalized and written off over their useful life. The depreciation so written off should be included as part of the expenditure on research and development and should also be included in the amount of depreciation disclosed under paragraph 12(1)(a) of the 2nd Schedule of the Companies Act 1967.

Exceptions

14. Where companies enter into a firm contract:

    (a) to carry out development work on behalf of third parties on such terms that the related expenditure is to be fully reimbursed; or
    (b) to develop and manufacture at an agreed price which has been calculated to reimburse the expenditure on development as well as the manufacture;

    any such expenditure which has not been reimbursed at the balance sheet date should be included in work in progress.

15. Expenditure incurred in locating and exploiting mineral deposits in the extractive industries does not fall within the definition of research and development used in this accounting standard.

Market research

16. The definitions of research and development expenditure, given in paragraph 18, are based on those used by the Organization for Economic Co-operation and Development and do not encompass expenditure on market research. Nevertheless the accounting treatment for expenditure on market research could generally be expected to follow that for research and development expenditure and thus it would generally be appropriate to write off such expenditure as incurred. Where market research is carried out to ascertain the factors set out in paragraph 8(b) in respect of a product which in all other respects satisfies the criteria set out in paragraphs 7–9

EXHIBIT 1.8 CONTINUED

itself, the related expenditure may reasonably be carried forward but should be separately disclosed.

Disclosure

17. The uncertainties inherent in development projects suggest that there is a case for disclosure for example of the nature, status and costs of individual research and development projects whether written off or not. It is however thought that to call for such detailed disclosure would raise considerable problems of definition. Accordingly, it is proposed that disclosure should be limited to the movements of unamortized development expenditure during the year.

Part 2 – Definition of terms

Research and development expenditure

18. For the purpose of this statement research and development expenditure means expenditure falling into one or more of the following broad categories (except to the extent that it relates to locating or exploiting mineral deposits or is reimbursable by third parties either directly or under the terms of a firm contract to develop and manufacture at an agreed price which has been calculated to reimburse both elements of expenditure):

(a) Pure (or basic) research: original investigation undertaken in order to gain new scientific or technical knowledge and understanding. Basic research is not primarily directed towards any specific practical aim or application.
(b) Applied research: original investigation undertaken in order to gain new scientific or technical knowledge and directed towards a specific practical aim or objective.
(c) Development: the use of scientific or technical knowledge in order to produce new or substantially improved materials, devices, products, processes, systems or services prior to the commencement of commercial production.

Part 3 – Proposed standard accounting practice

Accounting treatment

19. The cost of fixed assets acquired or constructed in order to provide facilities for research and development activities over a number of accounting periods should be capitalized and written off over their useful life.

EXHIBIT 1.8 CONTINUED

20. Expenditure on pure and applied research (other than that referred to in paragraph 19) should be written off in the year of expenditure.
21. Development expenditure should be written off in the year of expenditure except in the following circumstances:
    - (a) there is a clearly defined project; and
    - (b) the related expenditure is separately identifiable; and
    - (c) the outcome of such a project has been assessed with reasonable certainty as to:
        - (i) its technical feasibility; and
        - (ii) its ultimate commercial viability considered in the light of factors such as likely market conditions (including competing products), public opinion, consumer and environmental legislation; and
    - (d) if further development costs are to be incurred on the same project the aggregate of such costs together with related production selling and administration costs are reasonably expected to be more than covered by related future revenues; and
    - (e) adequate resources exist, or are reasonably expected to be available, to enable the project to be completed and to provide any consequential increases in working capital.
22. In the foregoing circumstances development expenditure should be deferred to the extent that its recovery can reasonably be regarded as assured.
23. The criteria for determining whether development expenditure should be deferred should be applied consistently.
24. Deferred development expenditure should be written off pro rata to the benefits expected to arise in future periods.
25. Deferred development expenditure should be reviewed at the end of each accounting period and where the circumstances which have justified the deferral of the expenditure (see paragraph 21) no longer apply, or are considered doubtful, the expenditure should be written off immediately.
26. Development expenditure once written off should not be reinstated even though the uncertainties which had led to its being written off no longer apply.

Disclosure

27. Movements on deferred development expenditure and the amount carried forward at the beginning and the end of the period should be disclosed.
28. Deferred development expenditure should be separately disclosed and should not be included in current assets.
29. The accounting policy followed should be clearly explained.

EXHIBIT 1.9 SSAP 13: ACCOUNTING FOR RESEARCH AND DEVELOPMENT (ISSUED DECEMBER 1977)

Part 1 – Explanatory note

[Paragraphs 1–10 and 12–17 are as in ED 17.]

11. If these uncertainties are viewed in the context of the concept of prudence, the future benefits of most development projects would be too uncertain to justify carrying the expenditure forward. Nevertheless, in certain industries it is considered that there are numbers of major development projects that satisfy the stringent criteria set out in paragraphs 7–9. Accordingly, where expenditure on development projects is judged on a prudent view of available evidence to satisfy these criteria, it may be carried forward and amortized over the period expected to benefit.

Part 2 – Definition of terms

18. The following definition is used for the purpose of this statement:

    Research and development expenditure means expenditure falling into one or more of the following broad categories (except to the extent that it relates to locating or exploiting mineral deposits or is reimbursable by third parties either directly or under the terms of a firm contract to develop and manufacture at an agreed price which has been calculated to reimburse both elements of expenditure):

    (a) Pure (or basic) research: original investigation undertaken in order to gain new scientific or technical knowledge and understanding. Basic research is not primarily directed towards any specific practical aim or application.
    (b) Applied research: original investigation undertaken in order to gain new scientific or technical knowledge and directed towards a specific practical aim or application.
    (c) Development: the use of scientific or technical knowledge in order to produce new or substantially improved materials, devices, products, processes, systems or services prior to the commencement of commercial production.

Part 3 – Standard accounting practice

Accounting treatment

19. The cost of fixed assets acquired or constructed in order to provide facilities for research and development activities over a number of accounting periods should be capitalized and written off over their useful life.
20. Expenditure on pure and applied research (other than that referred to in

EXHIBIT 1.9 CONTINUED

paragraph 19) should be written off in the year of expenditure.

21. Development expenditure should be written off in the year of expenditure except in the following circumstances when it may be deferred to future periods:

    (a) there is a clearly defined project; and
    (b) the related expenditure is separately identifiable; and
    (c) the outcome of such a project has been assessed with reasonable certainty as to:

        (i) its technical feasibility; and
        (ii) its ultimate commercial viability considered in the light of factors such as likely market conditions (including competing products), public opinion, consumer and environmental legislation; and

    (d) if further development costs are to be incurred on the same project the aggregate of such costs together with related production, selling and administration costs are reasonably expected to be more than covered by related future revenues; and
    (e) adequate resources exist, or are reasonably expected to be available, to enable the project to be completed and to provide any consequential increases in working capital.

22. In the foregoing circumstances development expenditure may be deferred to the extent that its recovery can reasonably be regarded as assured.
23. The criteria for determining whether development expenditure may be deferred should be applied consistently.
24. If development costs are deferred to future periods, their amortization should commence with the commercial production of the product or process and should be allocated on a systematic basis to each accounting period, by reference to either the sale or use of the product or process or the period over which the product or process is expected to be sold or used.
25. Deferred development expenditure should be reviewed at the end of each accounting period and where the circumstances which have justified the deferral of the expenditure (see paragraph 21) no longer apply, or are considered doubtful, the expenditure, to the extent to which it is considered to be irrecoverable, should be written off immediately.
26. Development expenditure once written off should not be reinstated even though the uncertainties which had led to its being written off no longer apply.

Disclosure

27. Movements on deferred development expenditure and the amount carried forward at the beginning and the end of the period should be disclosed.
28. Deferred development expenditure should be separately disclosed and should not be included in current assets.
29. The accounting policy followed should be clearly explained.

Date from which effective

30. The accounting and disclosure requirements set out in this statement should be adopted as soon as possible and regarded as standard in respect of financial statements relating to periods starting on or after 1 January 1978.

EXHIBIT 1.10 EXTRACTS FROM SUBMISSIONS TO THE ASC ON ED 14

Westland Aircraft Ltd

The treatment of [product development] expenditure in the . . . accounts is of great significance, because it has considerable influence on the profit percentage allowed in government contracts. This percentage is calculated by adding an agreed profit percentage on capital employed to the cost of the products. The calculation of capital employed is thus of great importance and it is agreed by HM government and the CBI that capital employed includes product development expenditure only if it is included in the company's balance sheet . . . Indeed the loss of profit could be as much as 40 to 50 per cent of the development cost if all the company's business is for HM government.

Whinney Murray (now Ernst and Whinney)

We consider that the proposed standard is likely to lead the practising profession into disrepute with our industrial counterparts who may have good reason to carry some development costs forward. A disservice will be provided to industry if the profession insists that development costs would be written off as incurred for reasons of accounting convenience and expediency. The matching concept is an important one and we do not believe that this should be surpassed [*sic*] by the prudence concept merely because of difficulties in obtaining a fair valuation for development costs.

(Both extracts are as quoted in Hope, T. and Gray, R. (1982) Power and policy making: the development of an R & D standard, *Journal of Business Finance and Accounting*, pp. 531-58.)

Case 2
Capitalization of Interest: Tesco

OBJECTIVES

1. To investigate the nature of the 'cost' of an asset.
2. To explore the problems involved in identifying how flows of resources within an organization are associated with each other.
3. To examine the impact of changes in accounting policy.
4. To investigate the difficulties which arise in interpreting interim financial reports.

MATERIALS

1. The interim report of Tesco plc for the six months ended 10 August 1985 (Exhibit 2.1).
2. Extracts from International Accounting Standard 23, 'Capitalization of borrowing costs' (Exhibit 2.2).

INTRODUCTION

The acquisition of a fixed asset may take place over a lengthy period, for example when a building is constructed under the supervision of the enterprise which is to use it, rather than being purchased from a construction company after completion. In addition to the costs of the tangible resources employed in constructing the asset, the enterprise will incur financing costs as a result of having to provide funds before the asset comes into use and generates revenue. These costs can be absorbed into the overall financing costs of the enterprise, and hence charged against revenue in the period in which they are incurred, or separated out and treated as part of the cost of acquiring the asset.

At the moment there is no UK standard dealing with this issue. International Accounting Standard 23, 'Capitalization of borrowing costs' (Exhibit 2.2), permits either method to be used but requires that the method chosen be used consistently. The Stock Exchange requires listed companies to disclose details of any interest capitalized. Tesco changed its accounting policy from writing off to capitalizing interest in its interim accounts for the six months to 10 August 1985 (Exhibit 2.1)

ANALYSIS

It is generally agreed that in arriving at the *cost* of a fixed asset, incidental expenses of putting the asset into a condition in which it can be used by the enterprise, such as delivery and installation charges, should be added to the purchase price of the asset itself. It is also generally agreed that the costs of financing an enterprise's operations should be charged in the period in which they are incurred rather than being allocated between the various activities – such as funding the holding of inventory – to which they relate.

These two principles come into conflict where fixed assets are acquired over a period of time so that an outlay of funds is required well before the point at which the asset can be brought into use. It can be argued that the cost of providing this finance for the period between the outlay and the asset coming into use is as much part of the cost of acquiring the asset as, say, expenditure on installing it. If this argument is accepted, the financing costs incurred during the period of acquisition – which will generally be the interest paid on the borrowings used to fund the acquisition of the asset – should be *capitalized*, that is, added to the capital cost of the asset (and thus included in the depreciation charge over its life) rather than being charged in the period incurred. If this is not done, the profit of the period in which the asset is acquired will be understated. A further argument in favour of capitalization is that if the asset had been acquired from a third party on completion, the purchase price would presumably have included an element to cover the cost of providing finance during construction, so that capitalization results in comparability between the costs of assets paid for in stages and those purchased by a single payment on completion.

The most significant technical problem in capitalizing financing costs is identifying the amount of such costs which should be capitalized. An enterprise will normally raise funds to finance its operations as a whole so that any attempt to associate the cost of a particular tranche of financing with the acquisition of a particular asset will inevitably be arbitrary. Even where a specific loan is raised to finance the acquisition of an identified asset, the finance could usually have been employed elsewhere in the organization, so that the opportunity cost of the finance may be the cost of a more expensive loan needed elsewhere because the finance used to fund the acquisition of the asset in question was thus not available for the alternative use. In principle, if financing costs are to be capitalized, it could be argued that this policy should be employed whether the finance is provided from loans or equity. In practice it is not normally possible to identify the cost of equity capital from objective evidence, and it is unusual for the cost of equity capital to be capitalized. As a result, physically indentical assets may be carried at substantially different amounts in the balance sheet, depending on how their acquisition was financed. A further argument against capitalization is that the income statement may give a misleading impression of the amount of borrowing costs incurred during a period.

QUESTIONS

1. Explain, giving reasons, whether you consider that borrowing costs associated with the acquisition of a fixed asset should be capitalized.
2. What difficulties, if any, do you think a financial analyst would encounter as a result of:

   (a) Tesco's policy on the capitalization of interest;
   (b) Tesco's change of policy;
   (c) the implementation of the change of policy in the interim accounts?

3. Exhibit 2.1 contains the whole of the financial information in Tesco's interim financial report. It complies with the relevant requirements of the Stock Exchange and few companies go much further in what they disclose. Would you, as a financial analyst, regard its contents as sufficient for your needs?

FURTHER READING

Anthony, R. N. (1975) *Accounting for the Cost of Interest*, Lexington Books, Lexington, Massachusetts.
Most, K. S. (1982) *Accounting Theory* (2nd ed), Ch. 9, Grid Publishing, Columbus, Ohio.

EXHIBIT 2.1 TESCO PLC: INTERIM REPORT

Consolidated Profit and Loss Account

	24 weeks to the 10th August 1985 £ millions	24 weeks to the 11th August 1984 £ millions	52 weeks to the 23rd February 1985 £ millions
Turnover including V.A.T.	1572.2	1397.6	3176.7
V.A.T.	86.6	73.9	176.3
Operating Profit	38.5	31.2	81.7
Interest receivable less payable (see Note 1)	5.7	(0.9)	(0.4)
Profit on ordinary activities before tax	44.2	30.3	81.3
Net margin	(2.98%)	(2.29%)	(2.71%)
Taxation (estimated)	18.0	12.0	30.3
Profit on ordinary activities after tax	26.2	18.3	51.0
Net surplus on sale of properties	2.5	3.4	8.7
	28.7	21.7	59.7
Dividend	8.6	5.9	16.4
Profit retained	20.1	15.8	43.3
Dividend per share	2.10p	1.75p	4.85p
Earnings per share (see Note 2):			
Excluding net surplus on sale of properties	6.96p	5.33p	14.84p
Including net surplus on sale of properties	7.63p	6.32p	17.36p

EXHIBIT 2.1 CONTINUED

Notes:

1. **Interest**
The cost of funding the store expansion programme now impacts substantially upon reported profit on ordinary trading activities. It has therefore been decided, with effect from 24th February 1985, to capitalise interest (net of taxation) on borrowings specifically related to the financing of the acquisition and development of new stores. Interest is being capitalised on store acquisition and development costs incurred in the current financial year and interest capitalisation will continue until these stores commence trading.

This has increased profit on ordinary activities before taxation in the current period by £3.5m and will have an increasing effect in the future. No adjustment has been made to the results for the previous year, as the amount involved was not material.

The proceeds of the rights issue made in April 1985 increased net interest receivable by approximately £2.9m.

Without the benefit of the above factors, the interest charge for the period would have been £0.7m, but now stands as a credit of £5.7m as a result of the capitalisation of interest and the interest on the rights issue proceeds.

2. **Earnings per Share**
Earnings per share for the 24 weeks to 11th August 1984 and for the 52 weeks to 23rd February 1985 have been adjusted to take account of the recent rights issue.

EXHIBIT 2.1 CONTINUED

Chairman's Statement

Trading Review

Our business has grown steadily and during the period turnover has been satisfactory, representing volume gain of approximately 7%.

The implementation of improved central distribution systems has continued, as have other productivity initiatives, which benefit net margin. Competition within the industry remains vigorous.

Store Development Programme

Nine new stores together with one major extension have been opened to date, increasing new selling area by 233,000 sq. ft. These, together with eight further stores to be opened during the financial year, will increase new selling area by 520,000 sq. ft. in total.

Eleven smaller stores have been closed this year to date, representing 155,000 sq. ft.

The 1986/87 store opening programme will continue at this substantial level.

Dividend

The Board, having considered the level of improvement in trading performance at the half year, has declared an interim dividend of 2.10p per share (1.75p last year), which will be paid on 21st February 1986 to shareholders on the register of members at the close of business on 17th January 1986.

Annual General Meeting

The full year's preliminary results will be announced on the 28th May 1986 and the Annual General Meeting of the company will be held on the 11th July 1986, both being two weeks earlier than in previous years.

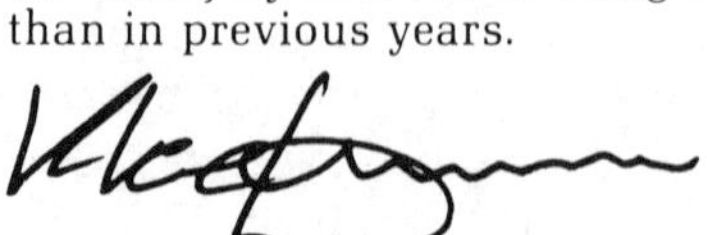

Ian C. MacLaurin
Chairman

18th November 1985

EXHIBIT 2.2 INTERNATIONAL ACCOUNTING STANDARD 23: CAPITALIZATION OF BORROWING COSTS

International Accounting Standard 23 comprises paragraphs 21–30 of this statement. The standard should be read in the context of paragraphs 1–20 of this statement and of the Preface to Statements of International Accounting Standards.

21. An enterprise that has incurred borrowing costs and incurred expenditures on assets that take a substantial period of time to get them ready for their intended use or sale should adopt a policy of either capitalizing borrowing costs or not capitalizing borrowing costs for those assets. The policy should be applied consistently in accordance with International Accounting Standard 8, 'Unusual and prior period items and changes in accounting policy'. Paragraphs 22 to 29 of this standard apply when a policy of capitalizing borrowing costs is adopted.

Capitalization of borrowing costs

22. Borrowing costs should be capitalized as part of the cost of an asset by applying a capitalization rate to expenditures on the acquisition, construction or production of assets that require a substantial period of time to get them ready for their use or sale.
23. The capitalization rate should be determined by relating the borrowing costs incurred during a period to the borrowings outstanding during that period. When a new borrowing is associated with expenditures on the acquisition, construction or production of specific assets, the capitalization rate may be determined on the basis of the actual borrowing costs incurred on that borrowing.
24. Capitalization of borrowing costs, for assets other than investments, should commence when:
    (a) expenditures for the asset are being incurred;
    (b) activities that are necessary to prepare the asset for its intended use or sale are in progress; and
    (c) borrowing costs are being incurred.

    Capitalization of borrowing costs for investments should commence when conditions (a) and (c) above are satisfied and the investee has activities in progress necessary to commence its planned principal operations.
25. Capitalization of borrowing costs should cease when the asset is ready for its intended use or sale or, in the case of investments, when the investee has commenced its planned principal operations. Capitalization should be suspended during extended periods in which active development is interrupted.

26. Where the construction of an asset is completed in parts and each part is capable of being used whilst construction continues on other parts, capitalization of borrowing costs should cease on each part as it is complete.
27. The amount of borrowing costs capitalized during a period should not exceed the total amount of borrowing costs incurred by the enterprise in that period. In consolidated financial statements, the limitation applied is the consolidated amount of borrowing costs.

Disclosure

28. The financial statements should disclose the amount of borrowing costs that have been capitalized during the period.

Transitional provisions

29. A change in accounting policy to comply with this standard should be applied to borrowing costs incurred in current and future periods and should be disclosed in accordance with the provisions of International Accounting Standard 8, 'Unusual and prior period items and changes in accounting policies'.

Effective date

30. This International Accounting Standard becomes operative for financial statements covering periods beginning on or after 1 January 1986.

Case 3
Goodwill: Greenwood

OBJECTIVES

1. To examine the nature of goodwill.
2. To investigate the impact of accounting standards.
3. To explore the difference between alternative accounting treatments which arrive at the same balance sheet total.

MATERIALS

1. Extracts from the annual report and accounts of Greenwood Services plc for the year ended 29 December 1985:
   (a) consolidated balance sheet at 29 December 1985 (Exhibit 3.1);
   (b) extract from the report of the directors (Exhibit 3.2);
   (c) extract from accounting policies (Exhibit 3.3);
   (d) extract from the notes to the accounts – note 8: Intangible fixed assets (Exhibit 3.4).
2. Extracts from SSAP 22:
   (a) definitions of 'goodwill' and 'separable net assets' (Exhibit 3.5);
   (b) standard accounting practice – paragraphs 28–38 (Exhibit 3.6).

INTRODUCTION

This case, unlike most in this book, is based on hypothetical data. Greenwood Services plc provides cleaning and catering services to hospitals and schools, and street cleaning and refuse collection services to local authorities. It has expanded rapidly in recent years, predominantly by taking over existing businesses, both incorporated and unincorporated. Often, one of the most valuable resources such businesses have is their existing contracts with clients, which may have several years to run. The existence of these contracts will be reflected in the price paid for the business; since they are not conventionally recognized as separable assets, however, there will be a 'gap' between the price paid for the business and the separable assets brought into the balance sheet. This gap is generally referred to as goodwill. In Greenwood's case, such goodwill amounted to some 21 per cent of its net assets (total assets less current liabilities) and this figure is by no means unusual in the services sector.

ANALYSIS

Viewed from a business perspective, goodwill can be attributed to such factors as a loyal and skilled work-force, good management, and established and satisfied customers who are more likely to go on buying an enterprise's products or services than to go elsewhere. In accounting terms, however, goodwill is the arithmetical difference between the 'value' of the business as a whole (as manifested, usually, by the price another enterprise has paid to acquire it) and the accounting 'value' attributed to all the other assets recognized in the group balance sheet. SSAP 22 adopts an accounting approach (see Exhibit 3.5).

Purchased goodwill arises when one enterprise acquires another as a going concern. Once it has arisen there are three basic accounting treatments available for it: it can be left permanently in the balance sheet (permanently capitalized); written off immediately, or amortized over a number of accounting periods. Until 1985 UK companies were free to adopt any of these alternatives. Under SSAP 22, however, permanent capitalization is not an acceptable treatment for accounting periods beginning on or after 1 January 1985.

In Greenwood's accounts for 1986, then, the accounting policy for goodwill will need to be changed if the group is to comply with SSAP 22. The obvious alternatives available to Greenwood are to write goodwill off against its accumulated profit and loss account, resulting in a deficit of £6,510,000, or to amortize it, with a consequent adverse effect on future profits.

A number of companies have shown a marked reluctance to adopt either of these two treatments. One favoured tactic for avoiding a write-off to the profit and loss account is to use the share premium account instead. An alternative is the creation of a separate 'zero' reserve against which goodwill is written off, so that there is, in effect, a 'dangling debit' in the capital and reserves section of the balance sheet. The use of the share premium account involves a rather elaborate procedure. Under the provisions of section 130 of the Companies Act 1985 the uses to which the share premium account may be put are severely restricted. However, on the basis of a special resolution by the company in a general meeting, confirmed by the High Court, the account can be cancelled and used to create a special capital reserve against which goodwill can subsequently be written off. In a number of cases the High Court has approved this use of share premium accounts. The procedure is not, however, costless because of the legal expenses that will be incurred. It should be noted that under either of the treatments outlined here the total capital and reserves of the company will be the same as if goodwill had been written off to the profit and loss account.

QUESTIONS

1. Indicate the effect on Greenwood's balance sheet and profit and loss account of treating goodwill as required by SSAP 22.
2. Explain the arguments for and against each of the methods you have considered in answering question 1.
3. What difference to your analysis of Greenwood's accounts would the choice of treatment for goodwill make?
4. Can Greenwood continue to include its intangible assets in its balance sheet without amortizing them and without breaching SSAP 22?
5. If Greenwood's accounts showed a true and fair view of its state of affairs at 29 December 1985, why should permanent capitalization be unacceptable on 30 December 1985?

FURTHER READING

Accounting Standards Committee (1980) *Accounting for Goodwill*, Discussion Paper, reproduced in *Accountancy*, August, pp. 108–20.

Holgate, P. A. (1985) *A Guide to Accounting Standards – Accounting for Goodwill*, Accountants Digest No. 178, Institute of Chartered Accountants in England and Wales, London.

Rutherford, B. A. (1981) Accounting for goodwill: the flaw in the 2½ × P/E rule, *Certified Accountant*, February, pp. 36-7.

EXHIBIT 3.1 GREENWOOD SERVICES GROUP: CONSOLIDATED BALANCE SHEET

Consolidated balance sheet at 29 December 1985	Notes	£000	1984 £000
Fixed assets			
Intangible assets	8	15,982	14,261
Tangible assets	9	39,988	34,620
Investments	10	16,956	20,288
		72,926	69,169
Current assets			
Stock	11	5,819	5,201
Debtors	12	33,463	31,672
Short-term deposits		1,725	2,109
Cash at bank and in hand		1,997	3,001
		43,004	41,983
Creditors: amounts falling due within one year	13	41,356	40,010
Net current assets		1,648	1,973
Total assets less current liabilities		74,574	71,142
Creditors: amounts falling due after more than one year	14	25,335	24,984
Provisions for liabilities and charges: deferred taxation	15	1,401	1,202
		47,838	44,956
Capital and reserves			
Called up share capital	16	18,970	18,970
Share premium account	17	16,810	16,810
Revaluation reserve	18	1,044	826
Profit and loss account	19	9,472	7,078
		46,296	43,684
Minority interests		1,542	1,272
		47,838	44,956

These accounts were approved by the board of directors on 8 May 1986
B. A. Greenwood: Director
C. F. D. Carpenter: Director

EXHIBIT 3.2 GREENWOOD SERVICES GROUP: EXTRACT FROM DIRECTORS' REPORT

Goodwill

The businesses of the group are based on long-term contracts with customers which carry an assurance of regular revenues for varying periods and offer the potential for renewal. There tends to be a pattern of renewals which further extends the expectation of regular revenues. Under these circumstances the directors consider that the amortization or writing off of the goodwill would not fairly reflect the value of the asset to the group; it is therefore carried forward unless there has been a permanent diminution in its value.

EXHIBIT 3.3 GREENWOOD SERVICES GROUP: EXTRACT FROM ACCOUNTING POLICIES

Goodwill

Goodwill represents the net excess of the purchase consideration paid for subsidiaries and other businesses acquired over the fair values of the net tangible assets acquired. It is carried forward unamortized unless the directors consider that there has been a permanent diminution in its value. Where a permanent diminution in value has occurred goodwill is written off against reserves.

EXHIBIT 3.4 GREENWOOD SERVICES GROUP: EXTRACT FROM NOTES TO ACCOUNTS

8. Intangible fixed assets

	Goodwill £000
At 31 December 1984	14,261
Exchange adjustments	1,369
Additions	1,734
Disposals	(430)
Written off against reserves	(952)
At 29 December 1985	15,982

EXHIBIT 3.5 EXTRACT FROM SSAP 22, PART 2

Part 2 – Definition of terms

21. *Goodwill* is the difference between the value of a business as a whole and the aggregate of the fair values of its separate net assets.
22. *Separable net assets* are those assets (and liabilities) which can be identified and sold (or discharged) separately without necessarily disposing of the business as a whole. They include identifiable intangibles.

EXHIBIT 3.6 EXTRACT FROM SSAP 22, PART 3

Part 3 – Standard accounting practice

General

28. No amount should be attributed to non-purchased goodwill in the balance sheets of companies or groups.
29. The amount to be attributed to purchased goodwill should be the difference between the fair value of the consideration given and the aggregate of the fair values of the separable net assets acquired.
30. The amount attributed to purchased goodwill should not include any value for separable intangibles. The amount of these, if material, should be included under the appropriate heading within intangible fixed assets in the balance sheet.
31. Purchased goodwill should not be carried in the balance sheet of a company or group as a permanent item.
32. Purchased goodwill (other than negative goodwill) should normally be eliminated from the accounts immediately on acquisition against reserves ('immediate write-off').
33. Any excess of the aggregate of the fair values of the separable net assets acquired over the fair value of the consideration given (negative goodwill) should be credited directly to reserves.
34. Purchased goodwill (other than negative goodwill) may be eliminated from the accounts by amortization through the profit and loss account in arriving at profit or loss on ordinary activities on a systematic basis over its useful economic life ('amortization'). When this treatment is selected, the following points apply:

    (a) Purchased goodwill should not be revalued. If there is a permanent diminution in value of purchased goodwill, it should be written down immediately through the profit and loss account to its estimated recoverable amount.
    (b) The useful economic life should be estimated at the time of acquisition. It should not include any allowance for the effects of subsequent expenditure or other circumstances subsequently affecting the company since these would have the effect of creating non-purchased goodwill.
    (c) The estimated useful economic life over which purchased goodwill is being amortized may be shortened but may not be increased.

35. Nothing in this standard precludes a company from using both the immediate write-off treatment and the amortization treatment in respect of the goodwill which relates to different acquisitions, so long as the accounting policies provide for the elimination of goodwill on a basis consistent with the standard.

EXHIBIT 3.6 CONTINUED

Treatment of existing goodwill

36. On the introduction of this standard, any existing positive goodwill carried in a balance sheet should normally, subject to paragraph 37 below, be written off directly against reserves. If the policy of amortization is adopted in accordance with paragraph 34 above, the company should, again subject to paragraph 37 below, calculate what the result would have been if the policy of amortization had been in effect from the date on which the goodwill was purchased. Any amount which would already have been written off by the date of introduction of this standard should be written off as a prior year adjustment; any balance should be amortized over the remaining useful economic life of the goodwill.
37. If a company has hitherto carried positive goodwill as a permanent item or adopted an amortization policy as from a date later than the date of its purchase, it may, irrespective of the policy for future purchases of goodwill, eliminate any positive goodwill carried in its accounts at the time this standard comes into effect by amortizing that goodwill prospectively (i.e. forward from the introduction of the standard) or, where a policy of amortization has already started, by continuing to amortize it. In each case the goodwill balance carried at the time this standard comes into effect should be amortized over not more than its remaining useful economic life. Where the treatment in this paragraph is adopted, no adjustment to the corresponding amounts is required.
38. A company may write off part of its existing goodwill in the normal way (that is, as set out in paragraph 36) and use the transitional provisions of paragraph 37 for the elimination of the remainder.

Case 4
Split Depreciation: Woolworth

OBJECTIVES

1. To investigate the nature of depreciation.
2. To investigate the relationship between the balance sheet and the income statement.
3. To examine the impact of revaluations on the historical cost system of accounting.
4. To consider the difficulty of achieving comparability between enterprises.
5. To explore the relationship between accounting standards and company law.

MATERIALS

1. Extracts from SSAP 12 (issued December 1977; November 1981 revision) (Exhibit 4.1).
2. Extracts from the annual report and accounts of Woolworth Holdings plc for the year ended 28 January 1984:

   (a) consolidated profit and loss account (Exhibit 4.2);
   (b) note 1: Accounting policies: depreciation (Exhibit 4.3);
   (c) note 2: Corresponding amounts: depreciation (Exhibit 4.4);
   (d) note 4: Depreciation (Exhibit 4.5).

INTRODUCTION

SSAP 12, which deals with accounting for depreciation, was first issued in December 1977. In the following year the European Community adopted the Fourth Directive on Company Law as part of its programme to harmonize the legal framework within which the commercial enterprises of the Community's member states operate. A Directive is an instruction to member states to amend their own laws to incorporate the provisions of the Directive. The Fourth Directive covered the preparation of financial statements; although it followed UK practice in one important respect – it contained an overriding requirement that accounts should show a true and fair view of the company's affairs – it generally adopted a continental European approach in that it contained detailed and prescriptive rules rather than setting down broad requirements and leaving the accounting profession to interpret them.

The UK implemented the Fourth Directive in the Companies Act 1981, which was subsequently consolidated with other companies legislation in the Companies Act 1985. The rules governing the form and content of accounts are to be found in Schedule 4. Section C of Part II provides 'alternative accounting rules' covering situations in which a company has revalued its assets, either systematically in the process of producing current cost accounts or on an *ad hoc* basis for inclusion in historical cost accounts. Paragraph 32(3), although worded in a rather ambiguous way, appears to allow what has become known as 'split depreciation'. This is the practice of continuing to base the depreciation charge in the profit and loss account on the historical cost of the asset after it has been revalued; the additional write-down necessary to achieve an appropriate net book value in the balance sheet is charged direct to the revaluation reserve. An example of the application of this policy is given in the next section.

Split depreciation was rarely, if ever, employed before the passage of the Companies Act 1981; thereafter it was adopted by a number of enterprises including Woolworth, which split depreciation in its financial statements for 1983/4 (see Exhibits 4.2 to 4.5) although it reverted to the orthodox treatment again in the following year.

In 1982 the ASC began a review of SSAP 12. An exposure draft of a revised standard (ED 37) was published in February 1985. Paragraph 16 of the draft required that, in order to achieve consistency between the profit and loss account and the balance sheet, 'the depreciation charge in the profit and loss account for the period should be based on the carrying amount of the asset in the balance sheet, whether historical cost or revalued amount'. A revised standard was likely to be adopted in the second half of 1986. The provisions relating to split depreciation are not expected to be different from those in ED 37.

ANALYSIS

The ASC's definition of depreciation is given in Exhibit 4.1. But what is the purpose of charging depreciation? It is sometimes suggested that depreciation is a kind of valuation technique, reflecting the extent to which the useful life of an asset has been exhausted and thus the consequential decline in its value. Considered as a valuation technique, though, depreciation is far from perfect since it fails to reflect increases in the price of new (and hence second-hand) assets. Another possible function is as a funding technique, ensuring that an amount equivalent to the cost of the asset is retained in the business over its life, thereby providing for replacement at the end of its life. However, the cost of replacing the asset (if it is replaced) will be unlikely to coincide with its original cost and, in any event, the funds retained as a result of charging depreciation are invariably invested elsewhere in the business so that they are not actually available when the need for replacement arises. A more modest claim for depreciation is that it is a technique for matching the cost of an asset with the revenue it generates.

The use of split depreciation can be demonstrated as follows. Consider the case of two indentical companies, A and B. Each has a fixed asset with an economic life of ten years and depreciates it on the straight line basis. The balance sheets of the two companies half-way through the life of their fixed assets are reproduced below.

	A	*B*
	£m	*£m*
Fixed asset		
Cost	10.0	10.0
Depreciation	5.0	5.0
	5.0	5.0
Other assets (net)	7.0	7.0
	12.0	12.0
Share capital and reserves		
Brought forward	10.0	10.0
Profit for the period	2.0	2.0
	12.0	12.0

Profit for the period is shown after deducting depreciation for the year of £1 million; no dividends were paid. Now suppose that company B revalues its fixed asset with effect from the *beginning* of the period. It considers that the market value of its asset is £9.6 million; hence the revaluation reserve will be entered in its books as follows.

	£m
Net revalued amount	9.6
Previous net book value (10.0 – 4.0)	6.0
Revaluation reserve	3.6

With company B's figures incorporating the revaluation, the financial statements of the two enterprises would now normally appear as follows.

	A £m	*B* £m
Fixed asset		
Cost or valuation	10.0	9.6
Depreciation	5.0	1.6
	5.0	8.0
Other assets (net)	7.0	7.0
	12.0	15.0
Share capital and reserves		
Brought forward	10.0	10.0
Revaluation reserve	—	3.6
Profit for the period	2.0	1.4
	12.0	15.0

Profit for the period is reduced for company B by £0.6 million because the depreciation charge is based on the valuation of £9.6 million and the remaining life of six years (£9.6 million × 1/6 = £1.6 million) rather than historical cost (£10 million × 1/10 = £1 million). Alternatively, the revalued asset could be shown at a gross value for a new asset (arrived at by reference to the valuation of the used asset and the extent to which its useful life has been exhausted – £9.6 million × 10/6 = £16 million) with accumulated depreciation (£16 million × 4/10 = £6.4 million) shown separately to arrive at the same net carrying amount.

The method known as split depreciation divides the total depreciation charge in B's accounts between the amount based on historical cost (£1 million) and the additional amount (£0.6 million) arising as a result of the revaluation. The latter amount is charged to the revaluation reserve leaving only the historical cost charge in the income statement. Under this method B's profit for the year would be the same as A's but the revaluation reserve would be reduced by £0.6 million.

The arguments in favour of split depreciation are that it provides a charge in the income statement which is comparable with that arising for enterprises with similar assets which have not been revalued; that it avoids the paradoxical situation in which an *appreciation* in the value of an enterprise's assets *reduces* its profits; and that profit does not vary according to the decision of the directors as to whether to incorporate a valuation into the financial statements. Opponents of split depreciation point out that it results in an inconsistency between the income statement and the balance sheet.

QUESTIONS

1. Do any of the following help to resolve the issue of whether split depreciation is appropriate and, if so, how?

   (a) the ASC's definition of depreciation;
   (b) an examination of the purpose of depreciation;
   (c) the requirement in SSAP 12 to allocate cost or revalued amount 'as fairly as possible'.

2. If the legislation allows split depreciation, should a standard seek to outlaw it?
3. Is consistency within a set of financial statements more important or less important than consistency between the financial statements of similar enterprises?
4. Should revaluation be permitted under the historical cost basis of accounting?

FURTHER READING

Nobes, C. (1985) *Depreciation Problems in the Context of Historic Cost Accounting*, Dartford, Certified Accountant Publications.

EXHIBIT 4.1 EXTRACTS FROM SSAP 12

Part 2 – Definition of terms

15. The following definition is used for the purpose of this statement: *Depreciation* is the measure of the wearing out, consumption or other loss of value of a fixed asset whether arising from use, effluxion of time or obsolescence through technology and market changes.

Part 3 – Standard accounting practice

Accounting treatment

17. Provision for depreciation of fixed assets having a finite useful life should be made by allocating the cost (or revalued amount) less estimated residual values of the assets as fairly as possible to the periods expected to benefit from their use.
21. Where assets are revalued in the financial statements, the provision for depreciation should be based on the revalued amount and current estimate of remaining useful life, with disclosure in the year of change, of the effect of the revaluation, if material.

EXHIBIT 4.2 WOOLWORTH HOLDINGS PLC:
CONSOLIDATED PROFIT AND LOSS ACCOUNT

Consolidated Profit and Loss Account

for the financial year ended 28 January 1984

	Notes	1984 £m	1983 £m (Note 2)
Turnover		1,268.6	1,124.0
Cost of sales		875.2	767.9
Gross profit		393.4	356.1
Other expenses less other income	3	331.7	309.4
Net interest payable	5	32.3	40.6
Profit on ordinary activities before taxation	6	29.4	6.1
Taxation on profit on ordinary activities	9	2.6	—
Profit on ordinary activities after taxation		26.8	6.1
Extraordinary income-surplus on disposals of land and buildings	10	36.0	26.7
Extraordinary charges	11	9.4	6.8
Extraordinary profit		26.6	19.9
Profit for the financial year	12	53.4	26.0
Dividends	13	5.5	4.6
Retained profit for the year	23	47.9	21.4
Earnings per share	14	39p	9p
Fully diluted earnings per share	14	33p	8p

EXHIBIT 4.3 WOOLWORTH HOLDINGS PLC: NOTE 1 TO ACCOUNTS

Notes to the Financial Statements

1. Accounting policies

Depreciation

Depreciation of fixed assets is calculated by the straight line method and the annual rates applicable to the principal categories are:

Land	– nil
Freehold buildings	– ¾%
Long leaseholds over 50 years	– ¾%
Short leaseholds 50 years and under	– over remaining period of lease
Landlord fixtures	– 4% or over remaining period of lease if less than 25 years
Tenant fixtures	– 10%
Computers	– 20%
Motor cars	– 25%
Commercial vehicles	– 33⅓%

Depreciation calculated on the cost to the group is charged in arriving at the profit on ordinary activities before taxation. Depreciation calculated on the difference between valuation and cost is deducted from the revaluation reserve.

EXHIBIT 4.4 WOOLWORTH HOLDINGS PLC: EXTRACT FROM NOTE 2 TO ACCOUNTS

2. Corresponding amounts

Depreciation

In previous years, the full amount of the depreciation charge each year, based on the revalued amount of the assets and subsequent additions at cost, has been included in arriving at profit on ordinary activities before taxation. The charge for depreciation is now split, with that part based on the revaluation excess being charged directly to the revaluation reserve. This change in policy has had the effect of increasing profit on ordinary activities before taxation by £1.8m. A similar adjustment has been made to the corresponding amounts, increasing the profit for the financial year ended 29 January 1983 by £1.8m.

EXHIBIT 4.5 WOOLWORTH HOLDINGS PLC: NOTE 4 TO ACCOUNTS

4. Depreciation		
Land and buildings	6.2	5.6
Fixtures, fittings and equipment	9.5	9.2
Assets leased to third parties	2.0	0.9
	17.7	15.7
Depreciation of land and buildings comprises:		
charged to profit and loss account	4.4	3.8
charged to revaluation reserve	1.8	1.8
	6.2	5.6

Case 5
Extraordinary Items and Prior Year Adjustments: Bemrose Corporation

OBJECTIVES

1. To consider the effect of extraordinary items on the reported performance of Bemrose Corporation Ltd.
2. To discuss the application of accounting policies by the Bemrose Corporation Board.

MATERIALS

1. Extracts from the annual report of Bemrose Corporation Ltd for the year ended 22 December 1980:

   (a) consolidated profit and loss account (Exhibit 5.1);
   (b) note 5: Extraordinary items (Exhibit 5.2);
   (c) principal activities – extract from directors' report (Exhibit 5.3).

2. Extract from SSAP 6, 'Extraordinary items and prior year adjustments' (issued 1974) (Exhibit 5.4).
3. Extract from SSAP 3, 'Earnings per share' (Exhibit 5.5).
4. Extracts from SSAP 6, 'Extraordinary items and prior year adjustments' (revised 1986) (Exhibit 5.6).

INTRODUCTION

One of the major problems in using an accruals-based accounting system which focuses on the results for a single year involves dealing with events which, due to their size or nature, might show an unrepresentative picture of an entity's performance. Suppose we take 'predictive ability' to be our criterion for preparing accounting reports. Then, if the reporting system were capable of providing sufficiently detailed information for a suitable number of time periods into the future, reporting events which by their size or nature are unusual would no longer present a problem. An existing equity investor, for instance, would simply discount the company's future net revenues at some appropriate rate. The resulting information would be one of the considerations in the investor's decision whether to sell, hold or increase the shareholding in question. (The other considerations would relate to the view the investor takes of the firm's future dividend policy, and factors influencing the firm's specific risk and overall market risk.)

However, such precise information about the future is not reported at present. We are compelled, therefore, to find a satisfactory means of making sure that events which are 'one-off' do not present an unfair picture of a company's affairs to the readers of its reports.

It could be argued that, provided sufficiently detailed information is published, the style of presentation and even the calculation of the final reported figures are unimportant. If the data is not in an acceptable form, it could be argued that the readers of accounts will simply make their own adjustments. Even though managements do appear to believe that investors are influenced by purely accounting changes which have no real economic impact, there is some evidence which suggests that stock markets tend not to be fooled by accounting changes having no real economic impact. For instance, Kaplan and Roll (1972) were not able to find a statistically significant relationship between earnings manipulation (through accounting changes) and security price movements. Although they found that security prices tended to increase around the date when a firm announced earnings inflated by an accounting change, they came to the conclusion that 'the effect appears to be temporary, and, certainly by the subsequent quarterly report, the price has resumed a level appropriate to the true economic status of the firm' (Kaplan and Roll, 1972, p. 245).

Does it matter, then, that firms might have a choice of accounting treatments available if there is little apparent long-term impact on security prices? A reduction in the variety of possible accounting treatments should benefit financial analysts, for instance, by reducing monitoring costs. In addition, investors are only one group of accounts users, others being, for example, employees, government, creditors, customers and suppliers. Can we be sure that these other groups are capable of making the necessary corrections to the accounting data to suit their own decision models?

ANALYSIS

SSAP 6, 'Extraordinary items and prior year adjustments', was issued in 1974 in order to resolve these issues. As regards the treatment of extraordinary items, there are two possible approaches to reporting company profits. The first approach, referred to by the Accounting Standards Committee as the 'current operating performance' approach, takes the view that the profit and loss account should include only those items which relate to the normal recurring activities of a firm. The essential point here is that the avoidance of distortion is crucial to a fair interpretation of the company's results. The second approach, referred to by the ASC as the 'all-inclusive' approach, is quite different. This approach takes the view that all events which occur over a period are useful in assessing a company's performance. If items are to be excluded because they are supposed not to be typical of a company's activities, these items have to be very precisely defined, otherwise subjectivity is introduced into the accounting process. The ASC has opted in favour of the 'all-inclusive' approach on the grounds that one of the main objectives of accounting standards is to narrow areas of difference and variety in accounting practice.

The importance of the definition of extraordinary items lies in the fact that paragraph 10 of SSAP 3, 'Earnings per share', defines earnings on the basis of consolidated profit of the period after tax and after deducting minority interests and preference dividends, but before taking into account extraordinary items (Exhibit 5.5). The earnings per share figure is generally believed to be an important indicator of a company's financial performance and of its dividend distribution policy, whilst the price/earnings ratio is believed to provide a useful indicator of profitability between different types of firm.

The definition of extraordinary items is provided in paragraph 11 of SSAP 6 (Exhibit 5.4). It should be noted that a separate category was created for 'exceptional items' which were to be included in the calculation of earnings per share, even though they were to be identified separately in the profit and loss account.

It should also be noted that, since extraordinary items are required to be shown in the profit and loss account after the company's charge for taxation has been deducted, it is therefore reasonable to show next to the extraordinary item the tax which is attributable.

Prior year adjustments were also referred to in SSAP 6 and were defined as arising from changes in accounting policies or from the correction of fundamental errors. It is not intended to discuss prior year adjustments further except to note that the accounting treatment is to show these items as movements on reserves rather than as entries in the profit and loss account.

During the early part of the 1980s the UK experienced a recession when a reduction in industrial output meant that many firms were forced to reduce their operations and lay off employees. As a result of this widespread process of reorganization, relatively large rationalization costs began to appear in the income statements of many companies.

In the case of Bemrose Corporation Ltd, the consolidated profit and loss account (Exhibit 5.1) shows extraordinary items amounting to £2,785,000. These relate to reorganization costs, fuller information being provided in note 5 (Exhibit 5.2). Due to falling demand, Bemrose Corporation took action to reduce manpower levels and to reduce capacity. It is appropriate at this point to refer to the principal activities of the group (Exhibit 5.3).

In 1980 the group decided to divest itself of all its book publishing activities with the exception of National Union Catalog, and of the extraordinary charge (£2,785,000), over £2,250,000 relates to book publishing. The remaining part of the extraordinary costs relate to packaging and transfer printing where both manpower and capacity levels were reduced. In other packaging areas the cost of redundancies amounted to £397,000 and these are represented by the exceptional item of that amount shown in the consolidated profit and loss account (Exhibit 5.1).

The original definition of extraordinary items in SSAP 6 was drawn fairly widely and, as a result, it seemed to many observers of financial reporting that the category of extraordinary items was being used too frequently. For example, some companies would report as extraordinary items costs which related to a reduction in operational activity. Now it could be argued that, in a competitive environment, many firms need to be flexible and able to respond to changing circumstances in order to survive. This necessarily involves moving out of those areas in which they no longer retain a comparative advantage, and is therefore a normal feature of their operations. But at what level should such rationalization costs be regarded as extraordinary items? One view is that, whereas rationalization costs associated with a continuing activity are not abnormal, the complete shutdown of a distinct activity or segment can be regarded as unusual and therefore an extraordinary item.

A revised version of SSAP 6 was issued in 1986. There are no major changes from the 1974 version, but two important modifications should be noted. First, the revised SSAP 6 (paras. 11-14) now provides a narrower definition of extraordinary items, particularly with regard to reorganization costs (see Exhibit 5.6). Note that the relevant provision is related to the *decision* to discontinue and not to the actual flows of expenditure. Thus, under SSAP 6, a company might report the full costs of closing a subsidiary as an extraordinary item in one accounting period even though that subsidiary could be fully operational at the balance sheet date and with no redundancies effected until the following period. Second, clarification of the term 'business segment' is provided in paragraph 32 of SSAP 6 (see Exhibit 5.6).

It is interesting to recall the original SSAP 6 definition of extraordinary items as being 'both material and expected not to recur frequently or regularly'. This wording has largely been retained in SSAP 6 (revised). Although some guidance is provided by examples of extraordinary items in paragraph 4 (Exhibit 5.6), nevertheless the absence of precise definitions for the terms 'material', 'frequently' and 'regularly' must mean a continuing reliance on subjective judgement and hence inconsistent treatment between companies.

QUESTIONS

1. Outline the main differences between the original and revised versions of SSAP 6.
2. Why is it believed that a standard for extraordinary items is necessary?
3. What are the effects of classifying an item as 'exceptional' rather than 'extraordinary'?
4. Would the accounting treatment for Bemrose Corporation have been different under SSAP 6 (revised)? How might the profit and loss account have been presented if the revised version had been in force in 1980?

REFERENCES

Accounting Standards Committee (1974) *SSAP 3: Earnings per Share*, ASC, London.

Accounting Standards Committee (1974) *SSAP 6: Extraordinary Items and Prior Year Adjustments*, ASC, London.

Accounting Standards Committee (1986) *SSAP 6: Extraordinary Items and Prior Year Adjustments*, ASC, London.

Kaplan, R. S. and Roll, R. (1972) Investor evaluation of accounting information: some empirical evidence, *Journal of Business*, April, pp. 225–57.

EXHIBIT 5.1 BEMROSE CORPORATION LTD: CONSOLIDATED PROFIT AND LOSS ACCOUNT

Consolidated profit and loss account

For the year ended 27 December 1980

	Note	1980 £'000	1979 £'000
Turnover		48 006	46 457
Profit before depreciation	[1]	3 457	3 564
Depreciation	[15]	1 365	1 287
Profit before exceptional costs		2 092	2 277
Exceptional redundancy costs		397	139
Trading profit		1 695	2 138
Interest	[2]	1 357	992
Profit before taxation		338	1 146
Taxation	[3]	77	206
		261	940
Preference dividends	[4]	11	11
		250	929
Extraordinary items	[5]	2 785	525
		(2 535)	404
Ordinary dividends	[4]	169	502
Transfer from reserves	[6]	(2 704)	(98)
Earnings per ordinary share of 25p	[7]	2.22p	8.26p

Note

The comparative figures have been restated to reflect the prior years' adjustment to which reference is made in notes 14 and 15.

EXHIBIT 5.2 BEMROSE CORPORATION LTD: NOTE 5 TO ACCOUNTS

	1980	1979
[5] **Extraordinary items**		
Provision for redundancies and other rationalisation costs:		
Already incurred	1 242	490
Expected to arise in the future	1 543	
Goodwill written off		35
	2 785	525

The costs expected to arise in the future relate to losses on disposals of stocks and fixed assets as well as other costs resulting from the decision to withdraw from the group's book publishing activities, other than the National Union Catalog. Whilst the costs expected to arise in the future, which it is anticipated will occur substantially in 1981, are of necessity difficult to quantify, and the eventual charge is likely to require adjustments, the Directors believe that the amount of £1 543 000 represents the best estimate which can be made at the present time. The provisions comprise £717 000 deducted from stocks, £197 000 from debtors, £44 000 from fixed assets and £585 000 (Parent £395 000) included in creditors.

The charge for extraordinary items would be reduced by £1 208 000 (1979: £255 000) had full provision been made for deferred taxation.

EXHIBIT 5.3 BEMROSE CORPORATION LTD: EXTRACT FROM DIRECTORS' REPORT

Principal activities

The principal activities of the group consist of packaging, printing (including security printing) and heat transfer printing.

As already referred to in the Chief Executive's review, the principal book publishing activities other than the National Union Catalog, are being discontinued.

EXHIBIT 5.4 EXTRACT FROM SSAP 6

Part 2 – Definition of terms

11. *Extraordinary items*, for the purposes of this statement, are those items which derive from events or transactions outside the ordinary activities of the business and which are both material and expected not to recur frequently or regularly. They do not include items which, though exceptional on account of size and incidence (and which may therefore require separate disclosure), derive from the ordinary activities of the business. Neither do they include prior year items merely because they relate to a prior year.

EXHIBIT 5.5 EXTRACT FROM SSAP 3

Part 2 – Definition of terms

Earnings per share

10. The profit in pence attributable to each equity share, based on the consolidated profit of the period after tax and after deducting minority interests and preference dividends, but before taking into account extraordinary items, divided by the number of equity shares in issue and ranking for dividend in respect of the period.

EXHIBIT 5.6 EXTRACTS FROM SSAP 6 (REVISED)

Extraordinary items

4. Extraordinary items are defined in paragraph 30. Extraordinary items derive from extraordinary events which are events outside the ordinary activities of the company. They do not include items of exceptional size or incidence which derive from the ordinary activities of the company. The classification of items will depend on the particular circumstances – what is extraordinary in one company will not necessarily be extraordinary in another because of differences in their ordinary activities. Similarly, what is extraordinary in a subsidiary company's own financial statements may not be extraordinary in the consolidated financial statements of that company's holding company. Subject to this, examples of extraordinary items could be material profits or losses arising from the following:

   (a) the discontinuance of a business segment, either through termination or disposal;
   (b) the sale of an investment not acquired with the intention of resale, such as investments in subsidiary and associated companies;
   (c) profits or losses on the disposal of fixed assets;
   (d) provision made for the permanent diminution in value of a fixed asset because of extraordinary events during the period;
   (e) the expropriation of assets;
   (f) a change in the basis of taxation, or a significant change in government fiscal policy.

This list of examples is not intended to be exhaustive.

Terminated activities

11. Where a decision has been made to discontinue a business segment, a provision is necessary for the consequences of all decisions taken up to the balance sheet date. This will usually include some or all of the following items:

   (a) redundancy costs (net of government contributions);
   (b) costs or retaining key personnel during the run-down period;
   (c) profits or losses arising from the disposal of assets, including anticipated ongoing costs such as rent, rates and security;
   (d) pension costs;
   (e) bad and doubtful debts arising from the decision to close;
   (f) all debits and credits arising from trading after the commencement of implementation;
   (g) any losses due to penalty clauses in contracts.

EXHIBIT 5.6 CONTINUED

12. Such provisions are not prevented from being treated as extraordinary items merely because they occur and are recognized over a number of accounting periods where this is either the ongoing result of a single decision or because of a number of separate decisions.
13. Profits or losses from terminated activities arising from trading before the commencement of implementation are part of the trading results for the year and are therefore not extraordinary. However, because these results derive from a business segment that has been discontinued, they may require separate disclosure to enable the results of continuing operations to be ascertained.
14. Programmes of reorganization which, although involving redundancies and a reduction in the level of activities, do not amount to the discontinuance of a business segment are not extraordinary. Such reorganizations are a normal business process and therefore form part of the ordinary activities of a company. Their costs are charged in arriving at profit or loss on ordinary activities, and shown as an exceptional item if material.

32. *A business segment* is a material and separately identifiable component of the business operations of a company or group whose activities, assets and results can be clearly distinguished from the remainder of the company's activities. A business segment will normally have its own separate product lines or markets.

Case 6
Extraordinary Items II: British Airways

OBJECTIVES

1. To consider the effect of extraordinary items on the reported performance of British Airways.
2. To discuss the application of accounting policies by the British Airways Board.
3. To examine the problems in determining performance of a nationalized industry in the period leading up to privatization.

MATERIALS

1. Extracts from the annual report and accounts of British Airways Board for the year ended 31 March 1982:

   (a) profit and loss accounts (Exhibit 6.1);
   (b) note 7: Extraordinary charges (Exhibit 6.2);
   (c) extract from accounting policies (Exhibit 6.3).

INTRODUCTION

The income statement of a nationalized industry represents a useful although by no means comprehensive picture of its performance over a period of time. It is generally accepted that over the years many nationalized industries have been subject to interference by governments in pursuit of their own political and economic objectives, and British Airways is no exception.

Because it is believed that reliance on the financial statements alone cannot provide a complete picture of the performance of a nationalized industry, it has been argued that additional indicators of performance should be published. Section 76 of the 1978 White Paper, *The Nationalized Industries*, refers to the need for performance indicators on the grounds that 'by themselves financial targets do not necessarily serve the purpose of stimulating management to greater efficiency, since to the extent that there is a monopoly situation the targets could be achieved by price rises or changes in the level of service'. Performance indicators are designed to provide extra information about productivity, efficiency and quality of service.

British Airways was formed in 1975 through a merger of British European Airways and British Overseas Airways Corporation, and over the years various governments have involved themselves in the investment decisions of British Airways and its predecessors. At times the airline has been persuaded to buy British-built planes rather than American aircraft as a result of the government's economic strategy. More recently the British Airways Board ordered Concorde against its commercial judgement, although it reached agreement with the government that it would receive compensation for losses incurred in its operation.

ANALYSIS

It is against this background that we should consider the possibility that the adoption of accounting treatments may be influenced by the government's objectives. There has been some debate in the accounting literature whether nationalized industries choose accounting policies which will further their own ends. Likierman (1983) has investigated a number of nationalized industries' accounting policies with regard to inflation accounting adjustments, and discusses the difficulties in proving manipulation.

When the government privatizes a state-owned industry and makes an offer of shares to the public and institutional investors, the price set for each share will be related to the view which potential investors are likely to take of the industry's prospects. A number of considerations need to be weighed up in determining a suitable share price. Setting too high an initial price will mean that those who took up the original offer will find that the share price will subsequently fall and their investment will fall in value. This will make it more difficult for the government to continue with its privatization programme. But offering what may be regarded as too generous a price is likely to incur charges from political opponents that the government is selling off the nation's assets 'too cheaply'. Moreover, the ability to set a relatively high price is attractive to government since it increases the receipts from privatization (thus reducing the public sector borrowing requirement).

If the government intends to maximize receipts on privatization, it would be keen to ensure that the accounts give a relatively optimistic view of the industry's future prospects and the ability to generate an acceptable return for future shareholders.

In 1981/2 British Airways put into operation a substantial programme of rationalization. It can be seen from Exhibit 6.1 that, during the financial year ended March 1982, more than £400 million was written off as extraordinary items. These items related to severance schemes and to write-offs of fixed assets, and the effect was to produce a 'bottom line' deficit of £545 million compared with a deficit of £145 million for the previous year. It is clear that the asset write-downs are related to the financial year in which the *decision* to rationalize was taken, and not to the financial years over which those assets were supposed to be losing their economic value. As regards the severance scheme costs, £100.4 million is for costs incurred to 31 March 1982 and £98.4 million is a 'provision for costs to be paid in completion of present schemes' (Exhibit 6.2). So it is likely that the major part of the latter figure relates to staff still employed during the following financial year (i.e. year ended 31 March 1983) and perhaps beyond.

It should be noted that, as a result of the 1981/2 extraordinary write-offs, there are several distinct effects upon the annual accounts for that year and also for subsequent years. First, the asset base is immediately reduced in value. Second, depreciation charges for 1981/2 and subsequent years will be reduced as a result of the asset write-offs, thereby reducing operating costs. Third, the reduction in numbers of employees will also mean that operating costs (i.e. staff salaries and wages) for future years will be reduced.

Finally, it is useful to consider the effect on a widely used indicator of financial performance, namely return on capital employed. This is usually defined as operating profit (i.e. profit after charging depreciation, but before charging interest and tax) divided by capital employed. It can be seen that if the extraordinary write-offs had not been made in 1981/2 but had been deferred to the next accounting period, or spread over a number of accounting periods, return on capital employed would have been markedly different.

QUESTIONS

1. Explain the impact of the extraordinary write-offs upon the annual accounts for 1981/2 and subsequent years.
2. Explain the impact of the extraordinary write-offs upon return on capital employed for 1981/2 and subsequent years.
3. In what ways might the accounting treatments adopted assist the government's privatization programme?
4. Discuss the view that for British Airways to report relatively large losses in 1981/2 would hinder, rather than help, the government's privatization programme.

REFERENCES

Likierman, A. (1983) Evidence on accusations of manipulating profitability: adjustments for inflation by the nationalized industries 1976–81, *Accounting and Business Research*, Vol. 14, pp. 29–34.

White Paper, (1978) *The Nationalised Industries*, Cmnd 7131, HMSO, London.

EXHIBIT 6.1 BRITISH AIRWAYS: PROFIT AND LOSS ACCOUNTS

Profit and loss accounts

	Note	Group 1982 £m	Group 1981 £m	Board 1982 £m	Board 1981 £m
Turnover	*1*	**2,241.3**	2,060.6	**1,924.7**	1,806.2
Operating surplus/(deficit)	*2*	**13.1**	(95.1)	**.9**	(108.7)
Subsidiaries	*11*			**2.6**	1.9
Associated companies	*3*	**4.9**	1.7	—	—
Trade investments	*4*	**.4**	.1	**.2**	.1
Other (charges)/income	*5*	**(7.6)**	23.4	**(9.0)**	11.8
Profit/(loss) before cost of capital borrowings and taxation		**10.8**	(69.9)	**(5.3)**	(94.9)
Cost of capital borrowings	*18*				
Interest		**(111.2)**	(73.1)	**(110.6)**	(72.7)
Currency (losses)/profits		**(13.3)**	2.3	**(13.3)**	2.3
Loss on ordinary activities before taxation		**(113.7)**	(140.7)	**(129.2)**	(165.3)
Taxation	6	**(5.4)**	(3.7)	**(1.3)**	(.4)
Minority interests		**.7**	(.7)		
Loss for the year before extraordinary charges		**(118.4)**	(145.1)	**(130.5)**	(165.7)
Extraordinary charges	7	**(426.4)**		**(407.0)**	
Balance transferred to reserves	*17*	**(544.8)**	(145.1)	**(537.5)**	(165.7)

EXHIBIT 6.2 BRITISH AIRWAYS: NOTE 7 TO ACCOUNTS

7	**Extraordinary charges**	Supplementary amortisation		
		Provisions to write down the unamortised cost of fleet and other assets to the amount estimated to be recoverable from future operations		
		Fleet	198.5	183.8
		Related property and equipment	9.4	6.9
			207.9	190.7
		Severance scheme costs		
		Net cost incurred to 31 March 1982	100.4	98.2
		Provision for costs to be paid in completion of present schemes	98.4	98.4
			198.8	196.6
		Provisions for other miscellaneous items	19.7	19.7
			426.4	407.0

EXHIBIT 6.3 BRITISH AIRWAYS: EXTRACT FROM ACCOUNTING POLICIES

AMORTIZATION AND DEPRECIATION

Amortization and depreciation charges are calculated on a straight line basis.

Fleet

Other than the aircraft fleets referred to below, owned aircraft and technical spares, together with aircraft held on finance leases where the option exercise price is nominal, are amortized at rates which are calculated to write down their cost to their estimated residual values on planned withdrawal from service or at expected date of disposal. Operational lives and residual values are reviewed annually in the light of experience and changing circumstances, and for these aircraft fleets currently range from ten to sixteen years with nil residual values. Leased aircraft where the option exercise price is other than nominal are amortized over the shorter of the primary lease period and the operational lives ascribed to owned aircraft of a similar type. Aircraft held on leases the terms of which require the Board to purchase the aircraft or make good any deficiency on disposal are amortized in line with the contractual arrangements.

The book value of the Concorde fleet was written down to nil in 1978/9 with the agreement of the Secretary of State for Trade. The net book value of subsequent capital expenditure on the Concorde fleet has been written down to nil at 31 March 1982.

The economic lives and residual values of the TriStar fleet have been reviewed in the light of the future availability of aircraft, spares and support for the operation of these assets, and their book values together with those of BAC 1-11, Trident, Boeing 707, Boeing V234 and Sikorsky 61N fleets have been

EXHIBIT 6.3 CONTINUED

written down to amounts estimated to be recoverable during their remaining lives. Trident and Boeing 707 fleets have been written down to nil at 31 March 1982 and the other fleets are being amortized over four to fifteen years to nil residual values.

Property and equipment

Provision is made for the depreciation of all property and equipment, apart from freehold land, based upon expected useful life and, in the case of leasehold properties, over the duration of the leases if shorter. Property and equipment related to aircraft fleets whose remaining lives have been reduced have been written down to the estimated recoverable amounts.

Case 7
Associated Companies: Lonrho/House of Fraser

OBJECTIVES

1. To investigate problems that arise in interpreting statements incorporating unorthodox accounting policies.
2. To contrast 'objective' and 'subjective' approaches to standard-making.
3. To examine an important case in the development of accounting standards.

MATERIALS

1. Definition of an associated company from the original SSAP 1 (issued January 1971) (Exhibit 7.1).
2. Definition of an associated company from the revised SSAP 1 (issued April 1982) (Exhibit 7.2).

INTRODUCTION

The definition of an associated company given in the version of SSAP 1 adopted in January 1971 (Exhibit 7.1) turns on the ownership of 20 per cent of the shares of the investee. The standard did not specify precisely what holdings should be counted as the group's in determining whether it held 20 per cent; in practice, however, this caused little difficulty for the first seven years of the standard's life. Groups included the shares owned by the holding company and its subsidiaries but excluded those owned by associated companies and companies held as trade investments.

In 1978 Lonrho, an international conglomerate, decided to include the shares it owned indirectly via its own minority investments in determining whether an investee counted as an associate. This policy was first employed in its interim accounts for the six months ended 31 March 1978. At that date, the company owned only 19.48 per cent of the shares in House of Fraser Ltd (HOF) directly; however, it also owned some 29 per cent of the shares of Scottish and Universal Investments Ltd (SUITS), which in turn had a 10.3 per cent interest in HOF. By including the shares in HOF attributable to its own holding in SUITS, Lonrho was able to argue that its holding in HOF amounted to 22.47 per cent.

The decision provoked a good deal of criticism in the financial press. In response, Lonrho placed an advertisement in a number of newspapers reporting that 'the company's joint auditors . . . have confirmed that, in their opinion, the treatment by Lonrho is in accordance with established accounting practice'.

By the end of the company's financial year, the disposition of holdings in HOF had not materially changed. Lonrho now held 19.1 per cent of the shares of HOF (via subsidiaries) and 29 per cent of the shares of SUITS, which in turn held 10.21 per cent of HOF. The same accounting policy was followed.

In the wake of the criticism of Lonrho's new accounting policy, the ASC embarked on a review of SSAP 1 and invited comments from members of the profession. Submissions were more or less evenly divided between those calling for a more rigorous objective test of substantial interest and those preferring a more flexible subjective test; both Lonrho's auditors (Peat Marwick Mitchell and Mann Judd) advocated flexibility although, in general, professional firms tended to prefer an objective test whilst companies argued for flexibility.

The ASC decided that revisions to SSAP 1 were required and in due course issued ED 25; on adoption as a standard the new version retained its original number. The new definition of an associated company is given in Exhibit 7.2. Ironically, although Lonrho would not have been able to include its indirect holding under the new definition, it would in fact have been able to adopt the treatment it did because of the relaxation in the 20 per cent criterion.

ANALYSIS

The definition of an associated company (other than in the case of a partnership) used in the original SSAP 1 contained four elements:

1. long-term interest;
2. substantial interest;
3. significant influence;
4. participation.

Three of these are to be determined subjectively, that is, by the judgement of those responsible for drawing up the accounts. For the fourth, substantial interest, the standard provides an objective test which operates quite independently of judgements by the preparers of the accounts about what constitutes a substantial interest: the test is simply whether 20 per cent of the investee's shares are owned by the group.

The principal attraction of an objective test is that it is easily validated and thus audited; it also produces results which have at least the appearance of consistency since groups with similar shareholdings will treat them in the same way. The main problem with an inflexible 'cut-off' point is that it may produce eccentric results at the margin: is a 19.9 per cent holding really not substantial when a 20 per cent holding is? Is it sensible for the acquisition of a single share to produce a major leap in the group's profits as an investment is switched from the trade investment to the associated company basis of consolidation?

The revised version of SSAP 1 employs an essentially subjective definition. Although 20 per cent is retained in the test, it is now a starting point for the exercise of judgement in deciding whether the presumption for associated company status created by a holding of that percentage is rebutted. The 20 per cent test is now to be applied in the context of 'significant influence' rather than, as before, of 'substantial interest'.

QUESTIONS

1. Do you think Lonrho's treatment of HOF complied with the version of SSAP 1 extant at the time? Give reasons.
2. Would your view of the situation have been different if Lonrho had owned 10.21 per cent of SUITS with SUITS owning 29 per cent of HOF?
3. Do you feel confident that, in analysing a set of accounts, you would appreciate the impact on the figures of the unorthodox accounting policy? What information would you need to evaluate the effect of the policy used by Lonrho in dealing with HOF?
4. Examine the changes in the definition of an associated company between the two versions of SSAP 1. What is the meaning of the change in the application of the 20 per cent criterion from a test of a 'substantial interest' to one of 'significant influence'?
5. Discuss the advantages and disadvantages of an objective test of associated company status.

FURTHER READING

Underdown, B. and Taylor, P. J. (1985) *Accounting Theory and Policy Making*, Ch. 11, Heinemann, London.

EXHIBIT 7.1 DEFINITION OF AN ASSOCIATED COMPANY FROM THE ORIGINAL SSAP 1 (ISSUED JANUARY 1971)

6. A company (not being a subsidiary of the investing group or company) is an associated company of the investing group or company if:

   (a) the investing group or company's interest in the associated company is effectively that of a partner in a joint venture or consortium; or

   (b) the investing group or company's interest in the associated company is for the long term and is substantial (i.e. not less than 20 per cent of the equity voting rights), and, having regard to the disposition of the other shareholdings, the investing group or company is in a position to exercise a significant influence over the associated company.

   In both cases it is essential that the investing group or company participates (usually through representation on the board) in commercial and financial policy decisions of the associated company, including the distribution of profits.

EXHIBIT 7.2 DEFINITION OF AN ASSOCIATED COMPANY FROM THE REVISED SSAP 1 (ISSUED APRIL 1982)

13. An *associated company* is a company not being a subsidiary of the investing group or company in which:

    (a) the interest of the investing group or company is effectively that of a partner in a joint venture or consortium and the investing group or company is in a position to exercise a significant influence over the company in which the investment is made; or
    (b) the interest of the investing group or company is for the long term and is substantial and, having regard to the disposition of the other shareholdings, the investing group or company is in a position to exercise a significant influence over the company in which the investment is made.

    Significant influence over a company essentially involves participation in the financial and operating policy decisions of that company (including dividend policy) but not necessarily control of those policies. Representation on the board of directors is indicative of such participation, but will neither necessarily give conclusive evidence of it nor be the only method by which the investing company may participate in policy decisions.
14. Where the interest of the investing group or company is not effectively that of a partner in a joint venture or consortium but amounts to 20 per cent or more of the equity voting rights of a company, it should be presumed that the investing group or company has the ability to exercise significant influence over that company unless it can clearly be demonstrated otherwise. For example, there may exist one or more other large shareholdings which prevent the exercise of such influence.
15. Where the interest of the investing group or company is not effectively that of a partner in a joint venture or consortium and amounts to less than 20 per cent of the equity voting rights of a company it should be presumed that the investing group or company does not have the ability to exercise significant influence unless it can clearly demonstrate otherwise. Unless there are exceptional circumstances, this demonstration should include a statement from the company in which the investment is made that it accepts that the investing group or company is in a position to exercise significant influence over it.
16. Where different companies in a group hold shares in a company, the investment in that company should be taken as the aggregate of the holdings of the investing company together with the whole of those of its subsidiaries but excluding those of its associates in determining whether or not significant influence is presumed to exist.
17. The term 'associated company' should be restricted to the definition given in this SSAP.

Case 8
Deferred Taxation: Marshalls Halifax

OBJECTIVES

1. To investigate the need for deferred tax accounting.
2. To consider the factors which have influenced deferred tax standards in the UK.
3. To contrast different methods of deferred tax accounting.

MATERIALS

1. Extracts from the report and accounts of Marshalls Halifax plc for the year ended 31 March 1986:

   (a) consolidated profit and loss account (Exhibit 8.1);
   (b) consolidated balance sheet (Exhibit 8.2);
   (c) notes on the accounts 1(e), 1(f), 6, 16, 18 and 23 (Exhibit 8.3).

2. Extracts from SSAP 15, 'Accounting for deferred tax':
   (a) basis of provision, paragraphs 6–12 (Exhibit 8.4);
   (b) method of computation and presentation, paragraphs 13–16 (Exhibit 8.5).

INTRODUCTION

Deferred tax is the term applied to potential taxation liabilities which are not likely to materialize for some considerable time into the future. For most companies this usually means at least two years ahead.

In order to understand why deferred tax provisions are considered necessary, it is important to distinguish between the terms 'profit before tax' and 'taxable profit'. Although they may appear to be synonymous there is a crucial distinction. 'Profit before tax' (usually described more fully as 'profit on ordinary activities before taxation') is the level of profit arrived at *after* deducting operating expenses (including depreciation) and interest but *before* deducting extraordinary items, dividends and (of course) tax. However, 'taxable profit' is the term applied to the figure which does not appear in the profit and loss account, or generally in the notes to the accounts, but which is used by the tax authorities as the basis for calculating tax payable.

The main reason why 'taxable profit' differs from 'profit before tax' is because in the UK the tax authorities ignore the depreciation charge which appears in the published accounts and apply instead their own rules for tax depreciation. For example, for a period of over ten years until 1984, companies could claim a 100 per cent tax allowance (known as a first year allowance – FYA) on purchases of plant and machinery. But in their published financial statements they would generally write off such assets at a much lower rate, over a longer period. The result was that there could be large discrepancies between the 'profit before tax' figure in the financial statements, and the 'taxable profit' figure.

Consider the following example.

A company whose financial year-end is 31 December bought a machine in 1979 for £100,000. It was depreciated over four years on the straight line basis with nil scrap value at the end of four years. No other fixed assets were purchased, and profits before tax in each of the four years beginning with 1979 were £80,000.

	1979	*1980*	*1981*	*1982*	*Total*
	£000	£000	£000	£000	£000
Profit before tax	80	80	80	80	320
Add back depreciation	25	25	25	25	100
	105	105	105	105	420
Less FYA	100	—	—	—	100
Taxable profit	5	105	105	105	320

It can be appreciated that, taking the four-year period as a whole, the profit before tax and the taxable profit are the same (i.e. £320,000). Thus, the differences for individual years are a matter of phasing or timing, hence the term 'timing differences'. It is of significant interest to the company since, under this system, it will pay its tax later than otherwise. Suppose that corporation tax were payable at the rate of 50 per cent on taxable profits; the tax payable on the 1979 profit would be only £2,500, but £52,500 for each of the years 1980 to 1982 inclusive.

Suppose now that the company were to purchase an additional machine in 1980, also costing £100,000. The new machine generates additional net revenues before depreciation of £25,000 per annum. It should be apparent that taxable profit would be £30,000 for 1980 but £130,000 for each of the years 1981 and

1982. Thus, the additional investment in machinery on a regular basis could delay the payment of much of the corporation tax – in some cases, depending on the scale of new investment, almost indefinitely.

Since the 1984 Finance Act, however, the system of company taxation has changed radically. Over a two-year period from 1 April 1984 first year allowances have been phased out. From 1 April 1986 an annual writing down allowance of 25 per cent on a reducing balance basis is available for plant and machinery. Hence, from 1984 onwards the discrepancy between a company's profit before tax and its taxable profit will gradually become less noticeable. In addition, the 1984 Finance Act eliminated stock relief and allowed for the corporation tax rate to be progressively reduced to 35 per cent for the year ended 31 March 1987.

Apart from these timing differences, other differences of a permanent nature can arise. These often occur because the tax authorities will not allow a particular type of expense to be deducted for tax purposes (for example, some types of entertaining expense incurred by firms). These differences are not a question of timing and are therefore ignored for the purposes of calculating deferred tax provisions.

ANALYSIS

There are essentially three ways of determining the tax charge reported in the profit and loss account (see Exhibit 8.4). One straightforward method, sometimes referred to as 'flow through' or 'nil provision', simply shows the tax liability which is directly payable as the result of the operations of a period. This method does not involve any provision for deferred tax. We could say that it fully accepts the tax authorities' way of calculating the tax payable. A second method, which is effectively in direct contrast to 'flow through', is the method referred to as 'full provision' or 'comprehensive allocation'. This method attempts to recognize *all* the tax effects of the operations of a period and rejects the tax authorities' way of calculating tax payable. The third method, 'partial provision', is a compromise between the first two and recognizes that under certain circumstances some tax liabilities will be deferred for such a length of time that their eventual payment may be postponed almost indefinitely.

Once it has been decided to make some form of provision for deferred tax, either full or partial, it is then necessary to decide on the method of computation (see Exhibit 8.5). There are two ways of calculating the provision – 'deferral' and 'liability'. They are not particularly helpful adjectives since both relate to the calculation of a deferred liability. Nevertheless, the deferral method has come to mean that the provision will be calculated on the basis of the tax rates in use when the provision was created. The liability method, however, will adjust the provision in the event that tax rates alter in the future. It can be seen that, provided tax rates do not change, there is no difference between the deferral and liability methods.

Recommendation N 27, 'Treatment of taxation in accounts of companies', published by the ICAEW in 1968, stated that distortions arising from timing differences 'should be avoided by providing for taxation on the accounting profit without regard to items allocated to other periods for taxation purposes. The difference between the corporation tax on the accounting profit and the corporation tax on the taxable profit should be dealt with through the deferred taxation account.' (ICAEW, 1968, para. 7.)

N 27 also recommended that the deferred tax should be calculated on what is now known as the 'liability' method, that is the deferred tax provision is adjusted in line with any changes which take place in the corporation tax rate. In addition, N 27 appeared to recommend what is now known as 'full provision' or 'comprehensive allocation': 'A deferred taxation account should be established and maintained at current rates of taxation whenever there exist material taxation liabilities which may crystallize at some future date on profits and surpluses already brought into account.' (ICAEW, 1968, para. 33.)

It was not until the Accounting Standards Committee was established and the publication of an exposure draft on deferred tax (ED 11 in 1973) that the controversy over a suitable standard for deferred tax began. Since 1973 there have been a number of changes in the approach adopted by the ASC. SSAP 11 was published in 1975, followed by ED 19 in 1977 and a new standard (SSAP 15) in 1978. Finally, a revised version of SSAP 15 was published in 1985 which took into account major changes to the tax system brought about by the 1984 Finance Act.

The revised version of SSAP 15 is substantially different from the original SSAP 11. Whereas SSAP 11 required full provision, SSAP 15 requires partial provision. Also, whereas SSAP 11 allowed either the deferral method or the liability method, SSAP 15 rejects the deferral method in favour of the liability method.

Hope and Briggs (1982) point out that many companies were unhappy with the original SSAP 11 since it would (and in the event did) lead to the creation of increasingly large deferred taxation provisions in company accounts. However, provided companies continued to invest on a regular basis, the liability could be postponed virtually indefinitely. One of the more persuasive arguments put forward by companies against SSAP 11 was that in the early 1970s the government had made a conscious decision to encourage investment and thereby boost growth in the economy by the introduction of 100 per cent tax depreciation. Yet the ASC was virtually attempting to negate this effect through SSAP 11 which seemed to suggest that companies were getting no material benefit from these very favourable allowances. If SSAP 11 had stood as it was originally published, the only way in which the benefit of these large tax allowances could be conveyed in the annual report and accounts would be by means of a cash flow report containing projections over a number of years into the future. Such a report would convey the fact that the company was gaining a considerable benefit by being able to delay tax payments and hence invest the resources for its own benefit.

Hope and Briggs analyse the development of the deferred tax standard in the context of the political issues raised. 'There has been increased recognition in the last few years by professionals and academics alike that accounting policy choices of measurement and disclosure should not be thought of as solely technical, neutral choices, but rather as political, social choices.' (Hope and Briggs, 1982, p. 83.) They take the view that many of the most important issues in the deferred tax standard are not simply technical issues which can be resolved by reference to an established framework. Instead, these issues can only be satisfactorily resolved by recognizing the political and social processes involved.

An opposing view to that outlined above is adopted by Solomons (1981) who considers that representational accuracy is an important concept in the preparation of financial reports, and draws an analogy between map-making and financial reporting: 'The better the map, the more completely it represents the complex phenomena that are being mapped. We do not judge a map by the behavioural effects it produces.' (Solomons, 1981, p. 148.) He concludes (at p. 151) that 'the criterion by which rules are to be judged is not the effect which they may or may not have on business behaviour. It is the accuracy with which they reflect the facts of the situation.' It is likely that Solomons would favour the original SSAP 11 on the grounds that it more closely relates the tax charge to the profits on which the tax liability is raised. In other words, the tax charge in the profit and loss account, so long as it contains a deferred tax element, will more closely represent the full taxation consequences of the trading operations of a particular year. It is, however, important to remember these two conflicting theoretical approaches when considering the issues involved.

The term 'foreseeable future' is not defined in the revised version of SSAP 15. Paragraph 28 of the standard states that the assumptions should be based on 'financial plans or projections covering a period of years sufficient to enable an assessment to be made of the likely pattern of future tax liabilities'. This is a less precise formulation than in the 1978 version of SSAP 15 which stated (in para. 28) that no deferred tax provision is necessary if:

(a) the directors are able to foresee on reasonable evidence that no liability is likely to arise as a result of reversal of timing differences for some considerable period (at least three years) ahead; and
(b) there is no indication that after this period the situation is likely to change so as to crystallize the liabilities.

The revised version of SSAP 15 refers (in para. 28) to the concept of prudence but only in relation to the probability that a liability will crystallize. It is interesting that later on, in paragraph 53, the standard states that 'The ASC has obtained legal advice to the effect that unprovided deferred tax is a contingent liability, except where the prospect of it becoming payable is so remote that it does not amount to a contingent liability at all.' The standard is almost on the point of addressing the notion of the time value of money. The value of SSAP 15 as a standard could possibly have been enhanced if there had been some discussion of the effect on the net present value of deferred tax liabilities given different rates of cost of capital, inflation and varying time spans. Certainly the justification for using the method of partial provision could have been made in these terms.

QUESTIONS

1. Explain the effects of a change in the corporation tax rates on the taxation charge of a company:
   (a) under the liability method;
   (b) under the deferral method.
2. Why is the taxation charge in the accounts of Marshalls Halifax not calculated as £2,875,200 (i.e. 40 per cent of £7,188,000)?
3. Contrast the three bases for calculating a company's tax charge. Outline the advantages and disadvantages of each.
4. What would happen if the tax rate from April 1987 onwards changed to 40 per cent?
5. What would happen if the tax rate from April 1987 onwards changed to 30 per cent?
6. Why is it useful for the user of accounts to have access to information about future capital commitments (see note 23 in Exhibit 8.3)?
7. What are the distinguishing features between 'permanent differences' and 'timing differences'?
8. What are the 'political' issues raised by the deferred tax standard?
9. What is the 'basis of provision' used by Marshalls Halifax?
10. What is the 'method of computation' used by Marshalls Halifax?

REFERENCES AND FURTHER READING

Hope, A. and Briggs, J. (1982) Accounting policy making – some lessons from the deferred taxation debate, *Accounting and Business Research*, Vol. 12, pp. 83–96.

Institute of Chartered Accountants in England and Wales (1968) *N 27: Treatment of Taxation in Accounts of Companies*, ICAEW, London.

Munson, R. J. (1986) Deferred taxation, in L. C. L. Skerratt and D. J. Tonkin (eds.) *Financial Reporting 1985–86: A Survey of UK Published Accounts*, Institute of Chartered Accountants in England and Wales, London.

Solomons, D. (1981) The politicization of accounting, in R. Bloom and P. T. Elgers (eds.) *Accounting Theory and Policy*, Harcourt Brace Jovanovich, New York.

EXHIBIT 8.1 MARSHALLS HALIFAX PLC: CONSOLIDATED PROFIT AND LOSS ACCOUNT

Consolidated Profit & Loss Account

for the year ended 31st March, 1986

	Notes	£000's 1986	1985
Turnover	2		
Concrete and quarrying		54,351	46,382
Engineering		14,990	14,588
		69,341	60,970
Operating profit	4		
Concrete and quarrying		6,816	5,782
Engineering		960	760
		7,776	6,542
Interest	5	588	574
Profit on ordinary activities before taxation		7,188	5,968
Taxation on profit on ordinary activities	6	2,529	1,055
Profit on ordinary activities after taxation		4,659	4,913
Minority interests		(1)	14
		4,660	4,899
Extraordinary items	7	115	42
Profit for the financial year	8	4,545	4,857
Preference dividends		101	101
Profit attributable to ordinary shareholders		4,444	4,756
Ordinary dividends	9	2,020	1,618
Retained profit	22	2,424	3,138
Earnings per share	10	12.11p	14.47p*

**adjusted for scrip issue*

EXHIBIT 8.2 MARSHALLS HALIFAX PLC: CONSOLIDATED BALANCE SHEET

Consolidated Balance Sheet

as at 31st March, 1986

	Notes		£000's 1986		1985
Fixed assets					
Tangible	11		30,561		26,099
Investment	12		22		22
			30,583		26,121
Current assets					
Stocks	13	17,120		13,630	
Debtors	14	13,551		13,427	
Cash at bank and in hand		157		38	
		30,828		27,095	
Prepayments and accrued income					
Advance corporation tax		839		763	
		31,667		27,858	
Creditors amounts falling due within one year	15	18,237		14,012	
Net current assets			13,430		13,846
Total assets less current liabilities			44,013		39,967
Creditors amounts falling due after more than one year	16	4,941		3,997	
Provision for liabilities and charges	18	428	5,369	400	4,397
			38,644		35,570
Capital and reserves					
Called up share capital	19		10,636		5,681
Share premium account	20		3,869		6,991
Revaluation reserve	21		3,169		3,199
Profit and loss account	22		20,867		19,595
			38,541		35,466
Minority interests			103		104
			38,644		35,570

Approved by the Board on 13th June, 1986
D R Marshall
K F Marshall
Directors

EXHIBIT 8.3 MARSHALLS HALIFAX PLC: EXTRACTS FROM NOTES ON ACCOUNTS

1 (e) Tangible fixed assets and depreciation

Tangible fixed assets are stated at cost, less any grants receivable, or professional valuation. With the exception of freehold and long leasehold land they are written off evenly over their expected useful lives.

The following rates are normally applied:

Freehold and long leasehold buildings	— 2½ to 5% per annum
Short leasehold property	— over the period of the lease
Fixed plant and equipment	— 8 to 25% per annum
Mobile plant and vehicles	— 14 to 30% per annum

Mineral deposits are depreciated on a royalty basis by reference to the tonnage extracted.

(f) Deferred taxation

Where it is considered that, due to differences between the treatment of items for accounts and taxation purposes, an additional liability will arise within the foreseeable future, provision for deferred taxation is made at the anticipated rate of corporation tax.

6 Taxation on profit on ordinary activities

	£000's	
	1986	1985
United Kingdom corporation tax at 40% (1985 — 45%) based on the profit for the year	**2,577**	1,372
Advance corporation tax	**(15)**	(120)
Overseas tax	**3**	2
	2,565	1,254
Prior year adjustments – Corporation tax	**(36)**	(199)
	2,529	1,055
The charge for United Kingdom corporation tax has been reduced due to the excess of capital allowances over depreciation by approximately:	**299**	1,272

16 Creditors amounts falling due after more than one year:

	Group £000's		Company £000's	
	1986	1985	**1986**	1985
Debenture (note 17)	**425**	447	**425**	435
Bank loans (note 17)	**2,785**	3,062	**2,775**	3,050
Taxation	**1,731**	488	**—**	—
	4,941	3,997	**3,200**	3,485

EXHIBIT 8.3 CONTINUED

18 Provision for liabilities and charges – deferred taxation

	£000's	
	1986	1985
Excess of capital allowances over depreciation	**428**	400
The maximum potential liability at 35% is:		
Excess of capital allowances over depreciation	**6,860**	6,520
Revalued properties	**1,243**	1,243
Losses available for set-off against future trading profits	**(51)**	(103)
	8,052	7,660
Advance corporation tax	**(839)**	(821)
	7,213	6,839

23 Capital commitments

	£000's	
	1986	1985
Capital expenditure for which no provision has been made in these accounts is:		
Contracted for	**3,320**	3,255
Authorised but not contracted for	**4,061**	4,947
	7,381	8,202

EXHIBIT 8.4 SSAP 15, PARAGRAPHS 6–12

Basis of provision

6. There are three principal bases for computing deferred tax.
7. The first is called 'nil provision' or 'flow through' and is based on the principle that only the tax payable in respect of a period should be charged in that period. No provision for deferred tax would therefore be made. Those who hold this view argue that any tax liability arises on taxable profits, not accounting profits, and therefore consider that it is necessary to provide tax only on taxable profits. Further, any tax liability arising on timing differences will depend on the incidence of future taxable profits and may therefore be difficult to quantify.
8. A basis radically different from nil provision is 'full provision', sometimes called 'comprehensive allocation'. This is based on the principle that financial statements for a period should recognize the tax effects, whether current or deferred, of all transactions occurring in that period.
9. An advantage of either of these bases is that the amounts involved can be precisely quantified. However, a crucial disadvantage is that they can lead to a purely arithmetical approach, in which certainty of calculation is given precedence over a reasoned assessment of what the tax effects of transactions will actually be.
10. The effect of timing and other differences on tax charges in relation to reported profits would be of little significance if taxation were not regarded as relevant to the performance of the enterprise for the period, and hence the only accepted indicator of performance were to be the result before tax. However, the result after tax is also widely regarded as an important indicator of performance and this will be distorted by accounting for deferred tax where it is probable that a liability or asset will not crystallize, or by failing to account for deferred tax where it is probable that a liability or asset will crystallize.
11. So far as the balance sheet is concerned, the amount of shareholders' funds and its relationship with the amount of funds from other sources may similarly be distorted by accounting for deferred tax where it is probable that a liability or asset will not crystallize, or by failing to account for deferred tax where it is probable that a liability or asset will crystallize.
12. A third basis is 'partial provision', which requires that deferred tax should be accounted for in respect of the net amount by which it is probable that any payment of tax will be temporarily deferred or accelerated by the operation of timing differences which will reverse in the foreseeable future without being replaced. Partial provision recognizes that, if an enterprise is not expected to reduce the scale of its operations significantly, it will often have what amounts to a hard core of timing differences so that the payment of some tax will be permanently deferred. On this basis, deferred tax has to be provided only where it is probable that tax will become payable as a result of the reversal of timing differences. Because it is based on an assessment of what will actually be the position, partial provision is preferable to the other bases described above.

EXHIBIT 8.5 SSAP 15, PARAGRAPHS 13–16

Method of computation

13. There are two principal methods of computation. The first is the deferral method, under which the tax effects of timing differences are calculated using the tax rates current when the differences arise. No adjustments are made subsequently if tax rates change. Reversals are accounted for using the tax rates in force when the timing differences originated, although in practice the effects of reversals and new timing differences are sometimes accounted for as one item. Those who support this method recognize that, when tax rates change, this method will not give an indication of the amount of tax payable or recoverable. Any deferred tax balance will therefore be a deferred tax credit or charge rather than a liability or asset. When tax rates change there is no need to revise the deferred tax already provided. Thus the tax charge or credit for the period relates solely to that period and is not distorted by any adjustments relating to prior periods.
14. The other method is the liability method, under which deferred tax provisions are calculated at the rate at which it is estimated that tax will be paid (or recovered) when the timing differences reverse. Usually the current tax rate is used as the best estimate, unless changes in tax rates are known in advance. As a result, deferred tax provisions are revised to reflect changes in tax rates. Thus the tax charge or credit for the period may include adjustments of accounting estimates relating to prior periods. The deferred tax provision represents the best estimate of the amount which would be payable or recoverable if the relevant timing differences reversed.
15. The liability method is the method consistent with the aim of partial provision, which is to provide the deferred tax which it is probable will be payable or recoverable.

Method of presentation

16. It is generally accepted that, however they have been calculated, tax effects should be shown in financial statements separately from the items or transactions to which they relate. An alternative would be to treat the tax effects of timing differences as integral parts of the revenue or expenditure, assets, provisions or liabilities to which they relate, rather than showing them separately. This 'net of tax' method recognizes that the value of assets and liabilities is affected by tax considerations, in particular tax deductibility. On the other hand, it fails to distinguish between a transaction and its tax consequences and therefore should not be used in financial statements.

Case 9
Source and Application of Funds: Bassett

OBJECTIVES

1. To consider the purpose of statements of source and application of funds.
2. To examine the problems involved in their use.

MATERIALS

1. Extracts from the report and accounts of Bassett Foods plc for the year ended 28 March 1986:
   (a) consolidated profit and loss account (Exhibit 9.1);
   (b) balance sheet (Exhibit 9.2);
   (c) source and application of funds (Exhibit 9.3);
   (d) notes to the accounts 2, 3, 5, 6, 8, 10–15 and 17 (Exhibit 9.4).
2. Extract from SSAP 10, 'Statements of source and application of funds' (Exhibit 9.5).

INTRODUCTION

The concept of financial statements showing movements of funds was formalized in the UK in 1975 with the introduction of SSAP 10, 'Statements of source and application of funds', although some companies had been producing such statements for several years previously.

SSAP 10 stresses that the statement of source and application of funds is not a replacement for the profit and loss account and balance sheet. These provide the data on which the movement of funds statement is based, the idea being that such a statement can provide additional insights into the financial performance of a firm. The information contained in the statement of source and application of funds is a 'selection, reclassification and summarization' (SSAP 10, para. 2) of the information in the profit and loss account and balance sheet.

The movement of funds approach represents a shift away from accruals-based accounting and attempts to identify movements which have taken place in a firm's resources. It is widely believed that companies which fail (especially those which fail through overtrading) suffer from a shortage of cash resources and access to credit rather than of accounting profit. SSAP 10 takes the view that by identifying movements which have taken place in assets, liabilities and capital, and changes in net liquid funds, one can gain a fuller understanding of a company's affairs.

The aim of SSAP 10 is to show how funds have been generated by the business as between its normal operations and other activities such as the sale of fixed assets or the issue of shares. It is intended to provide a link between the balance sheet at the start of the year, the profit and loss account and the balance sheet at the end of the year. The standard then requires the company to show how these funds have been applied, distinguishing between purchases of fixed assets and changes in working capital. The final figure to be shown is the change in *net liquid funds* which is defined by paragraph 8 as 'cash at bank and in hand and cash equivalents (e.g. investments held as current assets) less bank overdrafts and other borrowings repayable within one year of the accounting date'.

Other points worth noting are that a minimum of 'netting-off' should take place. For instance, sales and purchases of fixed assets, if material, should be shown separately. In addition, the figures in the funds statement should be identifiable in the balance sheet, profit and loss account, and notes to the accounts. In the case of group accounts, the effect of acquiring a subsidiary should be shown by way of a footnote to the statement.

Although SSAP 10 does not explicitly define the term 'funds', the standard provides three examples of movements of funds statements by way of an appendix, and each essentially uses profit before tax and after adding back depreciation as the basis for 'funds generated from operations'. It should be emphasized that the term 'funds generated from operations' is altogether different from the term 'operating profit'. 'Funds generated from operations' is based on a figure for profit *before* deducting depreciation but *after* deducting interest. 'Operating profit' is generally taken to mean a level of profit *after* deducting depreciation but *before* deducting interest.

ANALYSIS

Very few companies tend to publish more than two years' data on movement of funds. Given that movement of funds is not a complete accruals-based reporting system, it would seem useful if companies were to report data for, say, five years so that the reader would be in a better position to detect trends.

In the profit and loss account the charge for depreciation can be regarded as an indication of the wear and tear on fixed assets over a period of time resulting from their use by a firm. However, it does not provide a direct indication of the amounts invested in fixed assets during the year or an indication of any cash released by their sale. Although it is true that the use of an asset is likely to reduce the amount of cash ultimately realized on sale, provided no disposal has been made during the period no funds have been received.

The approach adopted by SSAP 10 is to take the profit before tax figure from the profit and loss account and then 'add back' the depreciation charge, describing depreciation as an item 'not involving the movement of funds'. It can readily be appreciated that, without some further explanation, the lay reader of accounts is likely to experience some difficulty in reconciling the notion of depreciation as appearing to be an addition to profit.

The reason why this rather cumbersome adjustment has to be made is because in the profit and loss account it is the convention to deduct from profit depreciation, interest and tax in that order. Since SSAP 10 does not show interest as an application, it follows that profit before interest cannot be shown as the source of funds. One solution would be to show interest as an allocation of funds. Profit before depreciation, interest and tax could then be used as the starting point for the movement of funds statement, and be easily identifiable with the same figure in the profit and loss account.

Incidentally, it should be noted that items in the profit and loss account sometimes described as 'profit/loss on sale of assets' simply reflect the fact that in previous years depreciation has been over- or under-provided. Such notional profits or losses do not in reality involve a movement of funds and it would seem to be consistent with the aims of SSAP 10 that these profits or losses should be shown alongside the depreciation charge for the year.

The figure for dividends also needs to be adjusted. Whereas the profit and loss account shows dividends as an appropriation of profit for the period, the statement of source and application of funds shows the dividends actually *paid*, irrespective of the accounting period.

One of the most important points to remember is that the starting point of the statement of source and application of funds is *profit before tax*. An appreciation of this point will considerably reduce the scope for confusion when interpreting movements of funds statements.

Profit before tax is a level of profit struck after deducting interest. It is reasonable to ask why the difference between interest accrued at the start and end of the period should not be shown as an item not involving the movement of funds. Interest paid is generally regarded as an item which is relevant to the interpretation of financial performance, and it is difficult to see why this expenditure is not shown as an application of funds along with dividends and taxation.

At this point the reader might well ask why similar adjustments to those outlined above for depreciation, tax and dividends are not made for other accruals-based figures, for example sales, purchases, interest, etc. This is not an easy question to answer.

One answer would be that if we made adjustments for all the accruals-based figures in the statement of source and application of funds we would simply be reversing all the accounting accruals involved in the preparation of the profit and loss account and balance sheet. In other words, we would end up with a straightforward cash flow statement – not what SSAP 10 seeks to achieve.

Another answer would be that we are obliged to accept that the definition of funds is somewhat arbitrary. It is as difficult to pin down a watertight definition of 'funds' as it is to define the term 'profit'. Consequently, for some elements of the statement of source and application of funds the accruals have been reversed, but for others they have not. It can be argued that this represents an inconsistent measurement approach.

It should be noted that the appendix to SSAP 10 is for general guidance and does not form part of the standard: 'The methods of presentation used are illustrative only and in no way prescriptive and other methods of presentation may equally comply with the accounting standard.' It is not surprising, therefore, that a wide variety of formats tend to be published (see, for instance, Brindle, 1984) and this does not help in trying to make intercompany comparisons.

It can be seen that the statement of source and application of funds represents a half-way stage between an accruals-based income statement and a purely cash-based cash flow report. Some writers have argued that the statement of source and application of funds represents a rather unsatisfactory hybrid of both statements. Mason (1983), for example, provides a useful analysis of the problems relating to the meaning of the term 'funds' and illustrates the confusion that can arise for accounts users in interpreting these statements.

QUESTIONS

1. On what grounds has SSAP 10 been criticized?
2. Trace, where possible, the data provided in Bassett's statement of source and application of funds for the year ended 28 March 1986 back to the balance sheet, profit and loss account and notes to the accounts. Comment on the treatment of the data. Specifically, explain the treatment of the following items:

   (a) depreciation (£1,643,000);
   (b) loss on disposal of tangible fixed assets (£57,000);
   (c) dividends paid (£933,000).

3. In what respects does the statement of source and application of funds for Bassett differ from the example provided in SSAP 10 (Exhibit 9.5)?
4. Does the statement of source and application of funds provide any information additional to that already contained in the balance sheet and profit and loss account?
5. What additional insights does the statement of source and application of funds provide?

REFERENCES AND FURTHER READING

Accounting Standards Committee (1975) *SSAP 10: Statements of Source and Application of Funds*, ASC, London.

Brindle, I. (1984) Source and application of funds, in L. C. L. Skerratt and D. J. Tonkin (eds.) *Financial Reporting 1984–85: A Survey of UK Published Accounts*, Institute of Chartered Accountants in England and Wales, London.

Mason, J. (1983) Funds statements: time to end the confusion, *Accountancy*, December, pp. 95–9.

EXHIBIT 9.1 BASSETT FOODS PLC: CONSOLIDATED PROFIT AND LOSS ACCOUNT

CONSOLIDATED PROFIT AND LOSS ACCOUNT

for the year ended 28th March, 1986

	Notes	1986 £000	1985 £000
Sales	1	69,579	69,352
Cost of sales		(48,545)	(47,109)
Gross profit		21,034	22,243
Distribution costs		(13.049)	(13.007)
Administrative expenses		(5,233)	(5,779)
Trading Profit		2,752	3,457
Interest	2	(899)	(617)
		1,853	2,840
Associate – share of loss		(4)	—
Profit before profit sharing and taxation		1,849	2,840
Allocation to employee profit sharing share scheme		—	(40)
Profit on ordinary activities before taxation	2	1,849	2,800
Tax on profit on ordinary activities	3	(351)	(165)
Profit on ordinary activities after taxation	4	1,498	2,635
Minority interests		(3)	(2)
Earnings		1,495	2,633
Extraordinary items	5	(443)	(394)
		1,052	2,239
Dividends – paid and proposed	6	(937)	(918)
		115	1,321
Earnings per ordinary share	7	10.94p	19.39p

Reserves		£000	£000
Opening balances		15,379	13,605
Transfer from profit and loss account		115	1,321
Retained profits – new subsidiary		—	494
Goodwill written off		(406)	—
Other movements on reserves		251	(41)
Closing balances	17	15.339	15,379

EXHIBIT 9.2 BASSETT FOODS PLC: BALANCE SHEET

BALANCE SHEET

at 28th March, 1986

	Notes	Group 1986 £000	Group 1985 £000	Company 1986 £000	Company 1985 £000
Fixed assets					
Tangible assets	8	17,659	16,622	114	110
Investments	9	19	—	5,346	5,330
		17,678	16,622	5,460	5,440
Current assets					
Stocks	10	11,261	11,176	—	—
Debtors	11	10,657	11,132	7,021	6,298
Cash at bank and in hand		862	195	4,078	4,181
		22,780	22,503	11,099	10,479
Creditors—amounts falling due within one year					
Bank loans and overdrafts	12	7,110	5,767	5,013	3,000
Trade creditors		7,782	6,188	—	—
Other creditors including taxation and social security	13	4,186	5,724	632	895
Proposed dividends		692	688	692	688
		19,770	18,367	6,337	4,583
Net current assets		3,010	4,136	4,762	5,896
Total assets less current liabilities		20,688	20,758	10,222	11,336
Creditors—amounts falling due after more than one year	14	(1,196)	(1,102)	(514)	(466)
Provisions for liabilities and charges	15	(607)	(752)	—	—
Minority interests		(18)	(16)	—	—
Net assets		18,867	18,888	9,708	10,870
Capital and reserves					
Called-up share capital	16	3,528	3,509	3,528	3,509
Share premium account	17	2,131	2,085	2,131	2,085
Revaluation reserve	17	340	343	—	—
Other reserves	17	926	478	—	31
Profit and loss account	17	11,942	12,473	4,049	5,245
Shareholders' funds		18,867	18,888	9,708	10,870

Signed on behalf of the board

H B Stokes
G R H Clemons } Directors

11th July, 1986

EXHIBIT 9.3 BASSETT FOODS PLC: STATEMENT OF SOURCE AND APPLICATION OF FUNDS

SOURCE AND APPLICATION OF FUNDS

for the year ended 28th March, 1986

	1986 £000	1985 £000
Source of Funds		
Profit on ordinary activities before taxation and after minority interests	1,846	2,798
Extraordinary items before taxation	(485)	(379)
	1,361	2,419
Adjustments for items not involving the movement of funds		
Depreciation	1,643	1,353
Share of loss of associate before taxation	4	—
Exchange valuation adjustments	(76)	(61)
Increase in minority interests	2	1
Loss on disposal of tangible fixed assets	57	148
Total generated from operations	2,991	3,860
Funds from other sources		
Sale of tangible fixed assets	513	237
Issue of share capital	19	377
Increase in share premium	46	54
Increase in creditors	249	672
Increase in development grants	67	76
Reserves of new subsidiary	—	494
Decrease in debtors	62	—
	3,947	5,770
Application of Funds		
Dividends paid	933	782
Tax paid less received	258	218
Purchase of tangible fixed assets	2,966	4,742
Goodwill on acquisition written off	406	—
Increase in stocks	85	1,617
Increase in debtors	—	1,115
Investment in associate	23	—
	4,671	8,474
Increase in bank overdrafts and borrowing less cash	(724)	(2,704)

Summary of the effects of the sale of SA Rouger et Cie and the acquisition of Anglo Bellamy Wilkinson Limited and Beech-Nut Sweets (England) Limited.

Net assets sold	£000
Tangible fixed assets	375
Stocks	150
Debtors	247
Creditors	(358)
Cash	2
	416
Loss on disposal	(381)
Proceeds of sale	35

Net assets acquired	£000
Tangible fixed assets	185
Stocks	225
Creditors	(15)
Cash	59
	454
Goodwill written off	406
Discharged in cash	860

EXHIBIT 9.4 BASSETT FOODS PLC: EXTRACTS FROM NOTES TO ACCOUNTS

NOTES TO THE ACCOUNTS

2. Profit on ordinary activities before taxation

Shown after charging (crediting) the following

	1986	1985
	£000	£000
Depreciation	1,643	1,353
Directors' emoluments As directors	3	3
As executives, (1985—including profit related incentive bonuses)	197	196
Charges for hire of plant and machinery	510	527
Audit fees	82	82
Interest on short and medium term borrowings	611	352
Interest on bank overdrafts	358	328
Interest received	(70)	(63)
Net interest	899	617

EXHIBIT 9.4 CONTINUED

3. Tax on profit on ordinary activities

The tax charge is based on the profit for the year and comprises:

	1986	1985
	£000	£000
UK taxation:		
Corporation tax at 40% (1985 – 45%)	339	171
Advance corporation tax	165	125
Deferred tax	(129)	(150)
	375	146
Corporation tax – prior year	(10)	—
	365	146
Overseas taxation:		
Current tax	11	6
Deferred tax	(25)	13
	(14)	19
Total tax charge	351	165

The UK tax charge for the year has been reduced by £271,000 (1985 – £1,076,000) in respect of losses brought forward and current year timing differences.

There are tax losses of approximately £10,000 (1985 – £850,000) available to be carried forward against future trading income.

5. Extraordinary items

	1986	1985
	£000	£000
Reorganisation costs	104	229
Loss on disposal of subsidiaries	381	150
Taxation on extraordinary items	(42)	15
	443	394

EXHIBIT 9.4 CONTINUED

6. Dividends

	1986	1985
	£000	£000
Ordinary		
Paid 3rd February, 1986:		
Interim of 1.78p (1985 – 1.68p)	243	228
Proposed: Final of 5.04p (1985 – 5.04p)	689	685
Preference	5	5
	937	918

As a result of the Finance Act 1972, dividends on the 7.5% cumulative preference shares are payable at the rate of 5.25% per annum.

8. Tangible fixed assets

(a) Movement in the year

		Group		Company
	Total	Land and buildings	Plant and vehicles	Plant and vehicles
	£000	£000	£000	£000
Cost or valuation				
Beginning of year	29,611	6,419	23,192	138
Additions	2,966	176	2,790	24
Disposals	(1,176)	(75)	(1,101)	(15)
Transfers	—	—	—	13
Reclassification	—	61	(61)	—
Exchange adjustment	641	181	460	—
End of year	32,042	6,762	25,280	160
Depreciation				
Beginning of year	12,989	1,910	11,079	28
Charge	1,643	134	1,509	26
Disposals	(606)	(20)	(586)	(9)
Transfers	—	—	—	1
Reclassification	—	2	(2)	—
Exchange adjustment	357	54	303	—
End of year	14,383	2,080	12,303	46
Net book value	17,659	4,682	12,977	114

EXHIBIT 9.4 CONTINUED

8. Tangible fixed assets

Land and buildings comprise:	£000
Freehold properties	4,382
Properties held on long lease	2,261
Properties held on short lease	119
	6,762

(b) Basis of valuation

Plant and vehicles and leasehold properties are shown at cost. The valuation of freehold property is as follows:

	£000
Overseas properties – directors' valuation at 2nd April, 1982	1,547
Cost	2,835
	4,382

Directors' valuations have been based on the appropriate professional advice.

Comparable amounts of freehold property determined according to the historical cost convention are:

	£000
Cost	3,757
Accumulated depreciation	1,391
Net book value at 28th March, 1986	2,366

(c) Incomplete capital expenditure

Included in the above is incomplete expenditure amounting to £988,000 upon which no provision for depreciation has been made.

(d) Capital commitments

At 28th March, 1986 the directors had authorised capital expenditure

	1986	1985
	£000	£000
against which orders had been placed	117	409
authorised but not committed	2,600	1,180
	2,717	1,589

EXHIBIT 9.4 CONTINUED

10. Stocks

	1986	1985
	£000	£000
Raw materials and consumables	3,925	3,816
Work-in-progress	953	948
Finished goods and goods for resale	6,383	6,412
	11,261	11,176

There was no material difference between the balance sheet value of stocks and their estimated replacement cost at the balance sheet dates.

11. Debtors—amounts falling due within one year

	Group		Company	
	1986	1985	1986	1985
	£000	£000	£000	£000
Due from subsidiaries	—	—	6,799	5,656
Trade debtors	9,048	8,715	—	—
Prepayments	693	798	178	332
Others	791	1,174	35	40
Taxation	125	445	9	270
	10,657	11,132	7,021	6,298

12. Bank loans and overdrafts

	Group		Company	
	1986	1985	1986	1985
	£000	£000	£000	£000
Short term bank borrowing in UK (unsecured)	4,500	3,000	4,500	3,000
Bank overdraft in UK (unsecured)	513	1,331	513	—
Bank overdrafts in overseas subsidiaries (secured)	2,097	1,423	—	—
Short term bank borrowing in overseas subsidiaries (unsecured)	—	13	—	—
Repayable within one year	7,110	5,767	5,013	3,000
Medium term bank borrowing: Repayable between two and five years (unsecured)	514	466	514	466
Repayable after more than one year	514	466	514	466
Total borrowing	7,624	6,233	5,527	3,466

EXHIBIT 9.4 CONTINUED

13. Other creditors including taxation and social security

	Group		Company	
	1986	1985	1986	1985
	£000	£000	£000	£000
Due to subsidiaries	—	—	44	255
ACT on dividends	386	662	386	392
Corporation tax	75	50	—	—
Overseas taxation	—	1	—	—
Value added tax payable	1,190	1,252	27	6
Social security and PAYE	449	588	32	61
Accruals and deferred income	2,086	3,171	143	181
	4,186	5,724	632	895

14. Creditors—amounts falling due after more than one year

	Group		Company	
	1986	1985	1986	1985
	£000	£000	£000	£000
Bank borrowing (see note 12)	514	466	514	466
Development grants	586	519	—	—
Corporation tax	96	59	—	—
Other creditors	—	58	—	—
	1,196	1,102	514	466

15. Provisions for liabilities and charges

The potential liability to deferred taxation, and the amounts provided are:

	Amounts Provided		Total Potential Liability	
	1986	1985	1986	1985
	£000	£000	£000	£000
United Kingdom:				
Capital allowances in excess of depreciation	2,889	3,380	4,016	4,663
Other timing differences	—	—	26	26
Losses	—	(295)	—	(320)
	2,889	3,085	4,042	4,369
Unrelieved advance corporation tax	(2,320)	(2,387)	(2,617)	(2,387)
	569	698	1,425	1,982
Overseas:				
Timing differences	38	54	289	281
	607	752	1,714	2,263

No provision has been made for taxation that would arise in the event of the overseas subsidiaries distributing the balance of their reserves.

EXHIBIT 9.4 CONTINUED

15. Provisions for liabilities and charges

The movements on the provisions for deferred taxation were:

	1986	1985
	£000	£000
Beginning of year	752	768
Profit and loss account	(154)	(137)
Disposal of subsidiary	3	—
New subsidiary	—	123
Exchange adjustment	6	(2)
End of year	607	752

17. Reserves

	Group			Company	
	Revaluation reserve	Other reserves	Profit and loss account	Other reserves	Profit and loss account
	£000	£000	£000	£000	£000
Beginning of year	343	2,563	12,473	2,116	5,245
Profit retained for the year	—	—	115	—	(1,196)
Foreign exchange translation differences	—	205	—	(31)	—
Increase in share premium	—	46	—	46	—
Transfer equivalent to depreciation on revalued assets	(3)	—	3	—	—
Disposal of subsidiary	—	243	(243)	—	—
Goodwill written off	—	—	(406)	—	—
End of year	340	3,057	11,942	2,131	4,049

EXHIBIT 9.5 EXTRACT FROM SSAP 10

Example 2

Groups Limited: Statement of source and application of funds

(Based on the accounts of the group and showing the effects of acquiring a subsidiary on the separate assets and liabilities of the group.)

	This year			Last year		
	£000	£000	£000	£000	£000	£000
Source of funds						
Profit before tax and extraordinary items, less minority interests			2,025			2,610
Extraordinary items			450			(170)
			2,475			2,440
Adjustments for items not involving the movement of funds:						
Minority interests in the retained profits of the year			25			30
Depreciation			345			295
Profits retained in associated companies			(40)			—
Total generated from operations			2,805			2,765
Funds from other sources						
Shares issued in part consideration of the acquisition of subsidiary*			290			—
Capital raised under executive option scheme			100			80
			3,195			2,845
Application of funds						
Dividends paid		(650)			(650)	
Tax paid		(770)			(970)	
Purchase of fixed assets*		(660)			(736)	
Purchase of goodwill on acquisition of subsidiary*		(30)			—	
Debentures redeemed		(890)			—	
			(3,000)			(2,356)
			195			489

EXHIBIT 9.5 CONTINUED

	This year			*Last year*		
	£000	£000	£000	£000	£000	£000
Increase/decrease in working capital						
Increase in stocks*		120			166	
Increase in debtors*		100			122	
Decrease in creditors – excluding taxation and proposed dividends*		75			17	
Movement in net liquid funds:						
Increase/(decrease) in cash balance*	(35)			10		
Increase/(decrease) in short-term investments	(65)			174		
		(100)			184	
			195			489

* *Summary of the effects of the acquisition of Subsidiary Limited*

Net assets acquired		*Discharged by*	
Fixed assets	290	Shares issued	290
Goodwill	30	Cash paid	60
Stocks	40		
Debtors	30		
Creditors	(40)		
	350		350

Case 10
Cash Flow Reporting: Whessoe

OBJECTIVES

1. To examine the case for cash flow reports.
2. To compare accruals-based and cash-based accounting systems.
3. To discuss the problems involved in preparing cash flow data based on published financial statements.

MATERIALS

1. Extracts from the annual report and accounts of Whessoe plc for the year ended 28 September 1985:
   (a) profit and loss account of the group (Exhibit 10.1);
   (b) statement of source and application of funds of the group (Exhibit 10.2).
2. Extracts from the annual report and accounts of Whessoe plc for the year ended 24 September 1983:
   (a) profit and loss account of the group (Exhibit 10.3);
   (b) statement of source and application of funds of the group (Exhibit 10.4).

INTRODUCTION

The reporting of information on a cash basis has been the subject of considerable debate in the accounting literature. The present position is that any cash flow data which is disclosed in the accounts of companies is done on a purely voluntary basis. It may be thought that the statement of source and application of funds is similar to a cash flow report, but it is important to stress that the statement of source and application of funds contains many accruals-based assumptions and the two should not be confused.

There are a number of arguments which have been advanced for and against cash flow reporting. Perhaps the strongest argument in its favour is that cash is such an important factor in determining a firm's prospects for survival that some information on cash flows is essential. It should be remembered that firms can fail, not through a lack of 'accounting profits' but from a shortage of cash. It is generally accepted that systems based on historic cost tend to provide an optimistic view of a firm's performance during a period of rising prices, and the use of cash flow reporting might, for example, make a company more cautious in its dividend distribution policy.

Second, it is argued that, by using cash flows, the allocation of revenues and expenses to distinct time periods is avoided. Cash flow systems do not involve the assumptions and conventions which are associated with the conventional system, such as the accruals and prudence concepts. For this reason it is argued that cash flow systems are more objective. Moreover, they are simpler and therefore easier to understand, particularly by readers of accounts who possess little formal accounting expertise.

It cannot be denied that cash flow systems do seem to avoid time period allocation, but one might reply that this does little more than throw the onus of making these allocations back on the reader. Consider the case of a firm which changes the credit terms for its customers in a particular year, so that they are required to settle their debts earlier than before. Under an accruals-based system it would in fact be easier to judge whether a lasting increase in sales had taken place since these would depend on evidence that the revenues had been 'earned', that is when a legal debt had been created or cash received. A cash flow system, on the other hand, would need further explanation to account for the change in the pattern of cash received. It could also be argued that cash flow systems do not satisfactorily settle the question of allocation but merely ignore it. Indeed, it has been argued that cash flow reporting does involve allocation in the sense that the basis of allocation is the date on which the cash flow arose. Accruals accounting, however, uses a criterion for allocation which normally depends upon estimates of consumption.

In some circumstances, using the date of payment or receipt as the basis of time period allocation may not be very helpful. Egginton (1984, p. 101) makes the point that 'the allocation could be determined by events which have nothing to do with the consumption of services, such as postal delays in the delivery of invoices'. It is also arguable whether cash flow reporting satisfactorily resolves the question of allocating flows to distinct headings such as capital and revenue. See, for instance, Rutherford (1982) and Egginton (1984). Such problems are common to both cash flow reporting and conventional accruals-based accounting. And it should be noted that if the emphasis of the reporting system is solely in terms of cash, some transactions may be missed altogether. For instance, a company may purchase fixed assets by issuing shares or may net off some debtors and creditors (Rutherford, 1982).

As regards the claim that cash flow reports are objective and, therefore, presumably less amenable to manipulation of the reported data, it should be pointed out that the management of a company could take action to 'improve' the reported figures, for instance by selling stock quickly at a loss. Under the accruals-based system it would be possible to inflate the sales figures by such a course of action, but an adverse effect would show up elsewhere, for instance in the profit margin. It is perhaps useful to distinguish between manipulations which are of an accounting nature and those which have a physical characteristic. Cash flow reports cannot be distorted by 'accounting' manipulations (for instance, changing the depreciation policy) but both cash flow systems and accruals-based systems can be distorted by 'physical' manipulations of the company's assets.

Third, whereas the traditional income statement reports only in terms of revenues and expenses, the cash flow report includes information related to new investment in physical assets and also information about changes in sources of finance. However, on its own a cash flow report cannot provide information about holding gains and losses and does not indicate how well or badly the assets of the company have been managed.

Fourth, accruals-based accounting systems incorporate estimates of future events into their data. For example, the calculation of a provision for bad debts will depend upon the view taken by the firm's accountants of the likelihood that certain debtors may eventually turn out to be bad. A straightforward cash flow report would avoid such estimates, since it would report only on the actual cash received from the firm's customers. However, the reader of a cash flow report who wants some idea of a firm's 'worth' at a point in time will need, as a separate statement, information about existing levels of debt and probability of eventual repayment.

One final point which needs to be made is that for a cash flow system to be fully effective, and in order to be able to identify trends, data over a number of previous years would be required and also cash flow projections for several years ahead. It is unlikely that companies will disclose cash flow projections on a voluntary basis and, therefore, some form of compulsion, either by way of statute or accounting standard would be necessary. There are still a number of problems to be overcome in implementing a comprehensive cash flow reporting system. Nevertheless, it does seem that the Accounting Standards Committee could usefully devote some of its resources to the issue of cash flow reporting rather than concentrating its energies exclusively on making incremental adjustments to the conventional reporting system.

ANALYSIS

It is possible to convert the data contained in published accounts to a cash flow basis. In doing this one is essentially reversing the original accruals calculations.

Lee (1981 and 1984), for instance, converted the data contained in the accounts of several large companies to a cash flow basis. One can start by referring to the statement of source and application of funds which generally shows some items of expenditure on a cash basis, for instance taxation and dividends. Some suitable measure of the cash flows generated directly by the company's normal trading activities is needed. Here we have to make some assumptions. We need to assume that changes in stocks, short-term debtors and short-term creditors relate entirely to trading operations. For our purposes we can refer to these three items as working capital, noting that this definition (for cash flow purposes) is different from the usual definition of working capital which includes cash at bank and in hand.

Following Lee (1981) we can calculate a figure for operating cash flow by taking the figure for funds from operations, then *deducting* any *increase* in working capital, or *adding* any *reduction* in working capital.

Calculating the other items in the cash flow report requires some care. Because the layout shown in SSAP 10, 'Statements of source and application of funds', is not prescriptive, some companies show sale proceeds on asset disposals while other companies report instead the net book value written off. In the case of Whessoe (Exhibit 10.2) it is clear that the company's policy is to deduct profit on disposal of assets (£68,000) in arriving at funds generated from operations (£6,175,000). The item 'sale of tangible assets' must, therefore, refer to sale proceeds.

It is assumed that purchases of tangible assets are made by cash or by long-term loans. If any finance for additional tangible assets is included in creditors due in less than one year, then our operating cash flow would be incorrect.

There is a variety of ways in which the cash flow report can be presented. One method of presentation adopted by Lee (1984) has essentially the following structure.

Example 10.1

Cash inflows	£
Operating cash flow	X
Additional borrowing	X
Additional share capital	X
	X
Cash outflows	X
Net investment	X
Tax paid	X
Dividends paid	X
Borrowing repaid	X
Cash balance increase	X
	X

In this statement it should be noted that operating cash flow is shown after deducting interest paid. The report would act as a master statement, and subsidiary schedules would elaborate on items such as net investment which is the net amount of purchases and sales of fixed assets.

An alternative method of presentation might be as follows:

Example 10.2

Finance	£
Increase in share capital	X
Increase in borrowing	X
Loans repaid	(X)
	X
Investment	
Sale of fixed assets	X
Purchase of fixed assets	(X)
	X
Operations	
Operating cash flow before interest	X
Interest paid	(X)
Taxation paid	(X)
Dividends paid	(X)
	X
Increase in cash	X

The purpose of the above statement is to show how much long-term finance has been raised and how it has been used in buying fixed assets. Next, information about the company's operations is shown. The crucial point here is that the company needs to ensure that its operating cash flow is sufficient to cover interest, taxation and dividends. Failure to do so over a prolonged period implies that the company must resort to borrowing to make these distributions.

QUESTIONS

1. Prepare a cash flow report for Whessoe for each of the four years to September 1985 on the basis suggested in Example 10.2.
2. Compare the cash flow information with the following profit and loss account information: turnover, operating profit, profit before tax, retained profit for year. What insights can thereby be gained into the company's performance? (For instance, comment on the company's dividend policy.)

3. Why might cash flow information in isolation be misleading to users of accounts?
4. What further information would be useful to a reader of cash flow reports?
5. Why are the cash flow figures you have calculated estimates rather than the 'true' cash flow data?

REFERENCES AND FURTHER READING

Egginton, D. A. (1984) In defence of profit measurement: some limitations of cash flow and value added as performance measures for external reporting, *Accounting and Business Research*, Vol. 14, pp. 99–111.

Lee, T. A. (1981) Cash flow accounting and reporting, in T. A. Lee (ed.) *Developments in Financial Reporting*, Philip Allan, Oxford.

Lee, T. A. (1984) SSAP 10 and cash flow analysis, *The Accountant's Magazine*, June, pp. 232–3.

Rutherford, B. A. (1982) The interpretation of cash flow reports and the other allocation problem, *Abacus*, Vol. 18, pp. 40–9.

EXHIBIT 10.1 WHESSOE PLC: GROUP PROFIT AND LOSS ACCOUNT 1985

WHESSOE

Profit and loss account of the Group

Notes	For the year ended	28th September 1985 £000	29th September 1984 £000
1	**Turnover**	99,981	99,679
	Cost of sales	88,588	89,697
	Gross profit	11,393	9,982
	Administration expenses	6,733	7,008
	Operating profit	4,660	2,974
	Share of profits of related company	489	659
2	Net interest	(124)	505
3	**Profit on ordinary activities before taxation**	5,025	4,138
4	Taxation on profit on ordinary activities	2,738	1,833
	Profit on ordinary activities after taxation, before extraordinary items	2,287	2,305
5	Extraordinary items	—	552
6	**Group profit for the year**	2,287	1,753
	Dividend—		
	Ordinary		
	Interim—2·5p per share (1984—2·5p)	452	452
	Proposed final—3·0p per share (1984—3·0p)	542	542
	Making a total dividend of 5·5p (1984—5·5p) per share for the year	994	994
19	**Retained profit for the year**	1,293	759
	Retained profit brought forward	18,113	19,340
17	Transfer to deferred taxation account	—	(1,986)
	Retained profit at 29th September 1984	18,113	17,354
19	Transfer to other reserves in the year	(1,000)	—
	Retained profit at 28th September 1985	18,406	18,113
7	Earnings per ordinary share of 25p	12·7p	12·8p

EXHIBIT 10.2 WHESSOE PLC: GROUP STATEMENT OF SOURCE AND APPLICATION OF FUNDS 1985

Statement of source and application of funds of the Group

	1985 £000	1984 £000
Source of funds		
Profit on ordinary activities before taxation	5,025	4,138
Extraordinary items (see note 5)	—	552
	5,025	3,586
Adjustments for items not involving the movement of funds		
Subsidiary company assets no longer consolidated	—	229
Profit on disposal of tangible assets	(68)	(18)
Related company	409	(368)
Depreciation, less capital grants released	1,716	1,453
Adjustment to past reserves due to exchange fluctuations	(907)	431
Profit on debentures redeemed	—	(5)
Total generated from operations	6,175	5,308
Funds from other sources		
Capital grants receivable	650	13
Sale of tangible assets	235	151
	7,060	5,472
Application of funds		
Dividend paid	(994)	(994)
Tax paid	(1,158)	(3,384)
Purchase of tangible assets	(4,925)	(3,103)
Debentures redeemed	(3)	(20)
Cost of acquisition of subsidiary	(250)	—
	(7,330)	(7,501)
	(270)	(2,029)
Increase (decrease) in working capital		
Stocks	676	2,640
Debtors	2,999	(2,725)
Creditors	444	3,911
Movement in net liquid funds:		
Decrease in cash at bank and in hand	(4,089)	(5,744)
Increase in overdrafts and loans	(300)	(111)
	(4,389)	(5,855)
	(270)	(2,029)

EXHIBIT 10.3 WHESSOE PLC: GROUP PROFIT AND LOSS ACCOUNT 1983

Profit and loss account of the Group

Notes	For the year ended	24th September 1983 £000	25th September 1982 £000
1	**Turnover**	111,353	98,175
	Cost of sales	99,908	86,572
	Gross profit	11,445	11,603
	Adminstration expenses	6,438	6,340
	Operating profit	5,007	5,263
	Share of profits of related company	792	485
2	Net interest	1,079	760
3	**Profit on ordinary activities before taxation**	6,878	6,508
4	Taxation on profit on ordinary activities	2,780	2,391
	Profit on ordinary activities after taxation	4,098	4,117
	Minority interest	—	(603)
	Profit before extraordinary items	4,098	4,720
5	Extraordinary items	271	710
6	**Group profit for the year**	3,827	4,010
	Dividend—		
	Ordinary		
	Interim—2·5p per share (1982—2·0p)	452	361
	Proposed final—3·0p per share (1982—3·0p)	542	542
	Making a total dividend of 5·5p (1982—5·0p) per share for the year	994	903
19	**Retained profit for the year**	2,833	3,107
7	Earnings per ordinary share of 25p	22·7p	26·1p

EXHIBIT 10.4 WHESSOE PLC: GROUP STATEMENT OF SOURCE AND APPLICATION OF FUNDS 1983

Statement of source and application of funds of the Group

	1983 £000	1982 £000
Source of funds		
Profit on ordinary activities before taxation, less minority interest	6,878	7,111
Extraordinary items (see note 5)	500	710
	6,378	6,401
Adjustments for items not involving the movement of funds		
Subsidiary company assets no longer consolidated	543	—
Loss on disposal of tangible assets	16	—
Related company	(397)	(66)
Minority interest	—	(340)
Depreciation, less capital grants released	1,659	2,116
Adjustment to past reserves	—	7
Profit on debentures redeemed	(3)	(304)
Total generated from operations	8,196	7,814
Funds from other sources		
Capital grants receivable	28	42
Sale of tangible assets	112	97
	8,336	7,953
Dividend paid	(994)	(813)
Tax paid	(1,356)	(932)
Purchase of tangible assets	(3,100)	(3,163)
Debentures redeemed	(8)	(663)
Repayment of EIB loan	(2,500)	—
	(7,958)	(5,571)
	378	2,382
Increase (decrease) in working capital		
Stocks	1,461	(609)
Debtors due within one year	(1,253)	(220)
Creditors due within one year	3,576	(7,126)
Movement in net liquid funds:		
Decrease in cash at bank and in hand	(4,122)	10,100
Decrease in overdrafts and loans	716	237
	(3,406)	10,337
	378	2,382

Case 11
Value Added: H. P. Bulmer Holdings

OBJECTIVES

1. To examine the case for value added reporting.
2. To discuss the problems involved in the preparation and interpretation of statements of value added.

MATERIALS

1. Extracts from the annual report and accounts of H. P. Bulmer Holdings plc for the year ended 25 April 1986:
   (a) five-year financial summary (Exhibit 11.1);
   (b) five-year added value statement (Exhibit 11.2).
2. Illustration of statement of value added from *The Corporate Report* (Exhibit 11.3).

INTRODUCTION

The popularity of the statement of value added appears to be largely due to the attention it received in *The Corporate Report*, published in 1975, although some firms had been publishing these statements for a number of years. The authors of *The Corporate Report* noted the 'trend towards the acceptance by business enterprises of multiple responsibilities and conclude that distributable profit is no longer the sole or premier indicator of performance in the corporate reports of such entities' (ASSC, 1975, p. 40). In particular, it was thought that employees could benefit from this statement and this has been argued subsequently in the literature, for instance by Cox (1979, p. 96) who writes: 'In changing to a value added format the door is opened for use of the figures for informing employees of the company's progress and generally for industrial relations purposes.'

The Corporate Report was a discussion paper and the statement of value added which is reproduced as Exhibit 11.3 was intended to be illustrative only. Most of the information is already published by companies in their consolidated profit and loss accounts, and the statement of value added essentially represents a rearrangement of this information. *The Corporate Report* suggested that alternative ratios based on value added could be calculated, and one of the purposes of the statement of value added is to adopt an entity approach to the firm as opposed to what can be called the proprietorial approach of the traditional income statement.

A particularly important (and debatable) view expressed in *The Corporate Report* is that management attitudes and objectives can be profoundly affected by changes in reporting practices. It also considers, as mentioned above, that for many organizations 'distributable profit is no longer the sole or premier indicator of performance' (ASSC, 1975, p. 40). But there are strong grounds to support the belief that management's freedom of action in allocating rewards amongst competing groups in a business enterprise is severely constrained. For instance, Watts and Zimmerman (1979) argue that if a manager is not maximizing the market value of a company's shares, that company is in danger of being taken over and the existing management replaced by others who will seek to increase reported profits, and thereby raise the share price.

Whereas *The Corporate Report* believes that changes in reporting practices can influence attitudes, Watts and Zimmerman (1979, p. 300) argue that 'The predominant function of accounting theories is now to supply excuses which satisfy the demand created by the political process.'

By the early 1980s a number of writers thought that there were benefits to be gained by allowing companies to continue experimenting with different accounting treatments and that a statement of standard accounting practice on the subject could be delayed. However, Rutherford (1980, p. 28) found that 'the extended period of experimentation has not yielded a substantially richer variety of treatments than was present in the first year, despite the very large increase in the number of statements published'. And in a survey of 300 large companies, Bougen (1983) found that the percentage of firms publishing the statement had declined to 21 per cent in 1982–3 from 29 per cent two years earlier.

The statement of value added seems to have been generally well received and there have been relatively few critics. Those who have criticized it have done so mainly on the grounds that the contentious term 'profit' is de-emphasized, and that retained profit is invariably shown under some such heading as 'reinvestment in the business' rather than as increasing a fund which will eventually be distributed to the shareholders. It has also been argued that publication of statements of value added might be in the interests of directors and shareholders since these statements obscure the conflict between wages and profits.

Perhaps one of the main conceptual difficulties with this statement is that it assumes a consensus model of industrial relations (i.e. the idea of a team working with common interests), whereas some would argue that in reality the interests of employees and management substantially conflict.

McDonald and Puxty (1979) take the view that the business organization is a coalition of interests and it is not conceptually justifiable to exclude customers and suppliers (which is effectively what the model in *The Corporate Report* does). This is a legitimate criticism. For instance, suppose we compare the roles of a supplier of goods and a bank. The supplier will be shown as a deduction from value added whereas the lender (i.e. the bank) will be shown as part of the 'team'. In practice the supplier could have just as much interest in the survival of the organization, if not more than the lender whose loan could be secured on the assets of the company and who would not lose out if the firm went into liquidation. The supplier, however, would be adversely affected by the loss of orders in the future. However, if all parties who have dealings with a firm are shown as part of the 'team' it can be seen that the statement of value added will simply become a list of the members of the team and the relevant values will merely add up to the total sales of the firm.

ANALYSIS

Some of the difficulties in interpreting statements of value added stem from the fact that the illustrative model in *The Corporate Report* did not provide more detail. Consequently, the heading 'bought-in materials and services' is often treated as a 'sink' for items of expenditure which could reasonably be treated instead as allocations of value added. Although there has been a fairly extensive discussion in the literature concerning the treatment of individual items of expenditure, companies do not appear to have taken this into account in preparing the statement. For example, depreciation can be treated either as a deduction from value added (the 'net value added' approach) or it can be excluded as in *The Corporate Report* illustration (the 'gross value added' approach). Morley (1978) provides strong arguments for the 'net' approach, yet about 80 per cent of large companies continue to use the 'gross' approach.

Should rent payable be classified as a bought-in service or should it be treated otherwise? Morley (1978) considers that if rent is treated as payment for the use of a factor of production, it would be consistent to show rent payable in the value added statement as an allocation to providers of capital. This method would also allow comparisons to be made more easily. For instance, a company which borrowed money to buy a factory would incur an increased interest charge which would be allocated under the heading 'to pay providers of capital'. Therefore it would be consistent to show rent payable by another company for a similar factory under the same heading. But in practice, the majority of companies classify rent payable as a bought-in service.

How should rates be treated? There are elements of the rates charge which are similar to a service, for instance the collection of refuse, so that classification of this item as a bought-in service would seem appropriate. However, rates are often considered to be a form of taxation collected by local rather than central government. There are strong arguments, therefore, for treating this item under the heading of 'to pay government'.

As a final illustration of some of the conceptual problems, how should bad debts be treated? One view would be that all the costs associated with bad debts, such as the write-off of the debt itself and collection expenses, should be treated as a bought-in service and therefore a deduction in calculating value added. However, non-payment of a debt should not hide the fact that value has been created. The point is that the value created has been appropriated by someone for whom it was not intended. It could then be argued that this expense should be shown as an allocation to an (unwanted) member of the team (i.e. the unreliable debtor). However, the model in *The Corporate Report* does not show customers as team members. Also, showing bad debts expense as an allocation rather than a deduction from value added could be confusing to readers of accounts, so at least on the grounds of pragmatism there are arguments for treating it as a deduction from value added.

QUESTIONS

1. In what respects does the five-year added value statement for Bulmer differ from the model in *The Corporate Report*? Comment on these differences.
2. Redraft the five-year added value statement of Bulmer in line with the model in *The Corporate Report* on:

   (a) gross basis;
   (b) net basis.

3. Compare the data in the published five-year financial summary with the data which you have calculated. What additional insights does the new information provide?
4. Should statements of value added be subject to an SSAP?
5. Discuss the arguments in favour of showing the following types of expenditure as allocations of value added rather than as a part of bought-in materials and services:

   (a) rent;
   (b) rates;
   (c) bad debts.

REFERENCES AND FURTHER READING

Accounting Standards Steering Committee (ASSC) (1975) *The Corporate Report*, Institute of Chartered Accountants in England and Wales, London.

Bougen, P. D. (1983) Value added, in D. J. Tonkin and L. C. L. Skerratt (eds.)

Financial Reporting 1983–84: A Survey of UK Published Accounts, Institute of Chartered Accountants in England and Wales, London.

Cox, B. (1979) *Value Added: An appreciation for the accountant concerned with industry*, Heinemann, London.

McDonald, D. and Puxty, A. G. (1979) An inducement-contribution approach to corporate financial reporting, *Accounting, Organizations and Society*, Vol. 4, pp. 53–65.

Morley, M. F. (1978) *The Value Added Statement*, Gee, London.

Rutherford, B. A. (1980) Published statements of value added: a survey of three years' experience, *Accounting and Business Research*, Vol. 11, pp. 15–28.

Watts, R. L. and Zimmerman, J. L. (1979) The demand for and supply of accounting theories: the market for excuses, *Accounting Review*, Vol. 54, pp. 273–305.

EXHIBIT 11.1 H. P. BULMER HOLDINGS PLC: FIVE-YEAR FINANCIAL SUMMARY

**H.P. Bulmer Holdings P.L.C.
and subsidiaries**

5 year financial summary

1982 £'000	1983 £'000	1984 £'000	1985 £'000	1986 £'000	Years ended April
					Net assets employed
26,994	32,054	42,739	60,445	57,488	Fixed assets
30,644	38, 540	43,332	59,032	62,603	Current assets
(19,824)	(24,367)	(26,826)	(47,734)	(52,286)	Current liabilities
10,820	14,173	16,506	11,298	10,317	Net current assets
(1,242)	(2,548)	(5,742)	(16,367)	(14,381)	Deferred liabilities
36,572	43,679	53,503	55,376	53,424	
					Financed by
2,593	2,593	2,593	2,593	2,593	Issued ordinary shares
32,613	39,720	28,798	30,671	28,719	Reserves
35,206	42,313	31,391	33,264	31,312	
1,366	1,366	22,112	22,112	22,112	Issued preference shares
36,572	43,679	53,503	55,376	53,424	Total shareholders' funds
71,317	89,382	102,783	124,665	138,148	**Net sales** (excluding tax and duty)
9,763	15,075	17,761	14,134	16,854	**Operating profit**
(1,890)	(1,142)	(964)	(2,892)	(4,429)	Interest payable
(361)	(618)	(708)	(386)	(621)	Employees' profit share
7,512	13,315	16,089	10,856	11,804	
—	—	—	(3,339)	—	Reorganisation costs
7,512	13,315	16,089	7,517	11,804	**Profit on ordinary activities before taxation**
6,148	10,316	11,473	6,945	7,507	**Profit on ordinary activities after taxation**
—	(816)	(2,282)	—	(2,411)	Extraordinary charges (Note)
6,148	9,500	9,191	6,945	5,096	**Profit for the financial year**
130	130	533	1,945	1,945	Preference dividends
1,307	2,178	2,541	2,541	2,745	Ordinary dividends
4,711	7,192	6,117	2,459	406	**Profit retained transferred to reserves**
					Profit on ordinary activities before taxation as % of:
20.5%	30.5%	30.0%	13.6%	22.1%	Shareholders' funds employed
10.5%	14.9%	15.7%	6.0%	8.5%	Sales
					Earnings per ordinary share:
11.6p	19.64p	21.09p	9.64p	10.72p	after charging reorganisation costs
			14.02p		restated to exclude reorganisation costs
3.6p	6p	7p	7p	7.5p	**Dividends per ordinary share** (gross equivalent amount per share)
					Dividend cover:
4.60	4.68	4.31	1.97	2.03	after charging reorganisation costs
			2.86		restated to exclude reorganisation costs

The summarised results for the years ended April, 1984 and 1985 have been restated to reflect the prior year adjustment to the deferred tax provision established as an extraordinary charge in the year ended April 1984 (see note 16 on page 34).

EXHIBIT 11.2 H. P. BULMER HOLDINGS PLC: FIVE-YEAR VALUE ADDED STATEMENT

H.P. Bulmer Holdings P.L.C.
and subsidiaries

5 year added value statement

Years ended April 1982 £'000	1983 £'000	1984 £'000	1985 £'000	1986 £'000	
71,317	89,382	102,783	124,665	138,148	Net sales
(45,973)	(56,641)	(64,684)	(86,553)	(97,721)	Bought in materials and services
—	—	—	(3,339)	—	Reorganisation costs
25,344	32,741	38,099	34,773	40,427	Total added value
					Comprising the following:
13,674	15,175	17,561	19,884	19,643	Employees' pay
361	618	708	386	621	Employees' profit share
1,890	1,142	964	2,892	4,429	Interest on borrowings
1,907	2,491	2,777	4,094	3,930	Depreciation of fixed assets
17,832	19,426	22,010	27,256	28,623	
7,512	13,315	16,089	7,517	11,804	Profit on ordinary activities before taxation
25,344	32,741	38,099	34,773	40,427	
7,512	13,315	16,089	7,517	11,804	Profit on ordinary activities before taxation
—	(816)	(2,282)	—	(2,411)	Extraordinary charges (Note)
7,512	12,499	13,807	7,517	9,393	Total profit
					This total profit has been applied:
1,364	2,999	4,616	572	4,297	To pay taxation
1,437	2,308	3,074	4,486	4,690	To pay dividends to shareholders
4,711	7,192	6,117	2,459	406	Retained to maintain and develop the business
7,512	12,499	13,807	7,517	9,393	
1,819	1,837	1,901	1,936	1,796	**Average number of employees in the group**
					Average amounts per employee in the group:—
£39,207	£48,657	£54,068	£64,393	£76,920	Net sales
£13,933	£17,823	£20,041	£17,961	£22,509	Added value
35.5%	36.6%	37.1%	27.9%	29.3%	as a percentage of net sales
£7,517	£8,261	£9,238	£10,270	£10,937	Employees' pay (excluding profit share)
19.2%	17.0%	17.1%	16.0%	14.2%	as a percentage of net sales
£4,130	£7,248	£8,463	£3,883	£6,572	Profit on ordinary activities before taxation
10.5%	14.9%	15.7%	6.0%	8.5%	as a percentage of net sales
£2,590	£3,915	£3,218	£1,270	£226	Profit retained
6.6%	8.0%	6.0%	2.0%	0.3%	as a percentage of net sales

The added value statement for the year ended April, 1984 has been restated to reflect the prior year adjustment to the deferred tax provision established as an extraordinary charge in that year (see note 16 on page 34).

EXHIBIT 11.3 ILLUSTRATION OF STATEMENT OF VALUE ADDED

Illustration

A manufacturing company
Statement of value added

		Year to 31 Dec 1974		Preceding Year
		£M		£M
Turnover		103.9		102.3
Bought-in materials and services		67.6		72.1
Value added		£36.3		£30.2
Applied the following way				
To pay employees				
wages, pensions and fringe benefits		25.9		17.3
To pay providers of capital				
interest on loans	0.8		0.6	
dividends to shareholders	0.9		0.9	
		1.7		1.5
To pay government				
corporation tax payable		3.9		3.1
To provide for maintenance and expansion of assets				
depreciation	2.0		1.8	
retained profits	2.8		6.5	
		4.8		8.3
Value added		£36.3		£30.2

Source: ASSC, *The Corporate Report* (1975).

Case 12
Segmental Reporting: Reed International

OBJECTIVES

1. To investigate the difficulties that arise in producing financial reports for diversified enterprises.
2. To explore the treatment of internal sales and common costs as examples of the allocation problem.
3. To examine the problems caused by the absence of an accounting standard.
4. To contrast formal financial statements with 'informal' commentaries as a means of conveying financial information.

MATERIALS

1. Extract from the Companies Act 1985 (Exhibit 12.1).
2. Extract from the Stock Exchange continuing obligations for companies (Exhibit 12.2).
3. Extracts from International Accounting Standard 14, 'Reporting financial information by segment' (Exhibit 12.3).
4. Extracts from the annual report and accounts of Reed International plc for the year ended 31 March 1985:

   (a) consolidated profit and loss account (Exhibit 12.4);
   (b) note 26: Analysis of turnover and profit (Exhibit 12.5);
   (c) operating group review: Paint and DIY (Exhibit 12.6).

INTRODUCTION

Company law has since 1967 required companies to disclose turnover and profits broken down by class of business where two or more substantially different classes of business are carried on (Exhibit 12.1), and the Stock Exchange imposes additional requirements for segmental information in respect of listed companies (Exhibit 12.2). However, there is as yet no UK standard covering segmental reporting although the International Accounting Standards Committee has issued one (Exhibit 12.3).

The report of Reed International provides a good example of the standard of disclosure reached by the more forthcoming large and diversified listed companies. Information is given both in the main accounts and in the commentary accompanying the accounts (Exhibits 12.4 to 12.6).

ANALYSIS

Much of the work of the financial analyst consists of making comparisons. The results and position of an enterprise operating in a single industry can be compared relatively easily with the performance both of other enterprises in the same industry and of the industry as a whole. Such comparisons are often necessary when evaluating, for example, the quality of management talent: a management which merely breaks even in a period when its competitors are making substantial losses has performed well – despite appearances – and may also be expected to beat the average when the industry recovers.

However, when a company diversifies into two or more industries it is no longer possible to compare its overall performance with that of other enterprises – unless another company happens to have diversified into the same industries and in the same proportions. In order to restore comparability it is necessary for analysts – and other users of the accounts – to have information disaggregated between the sectors in which the enterprise operates. Only in this way can the performance of the company be related to that of similar enterprises. It may also be necessary to know in which industries an enterprise is operating to assess, for example, its future prospects and opportunities for growth. Much the same argument applies to companies which diversify across two or more geographical regions, since profitability and other aspects of performance may vary by region as well as by industrial sector.

There would be no difficulty in producing segmental financial statements if a diversified enterprise consisted of a number of completely independent operations – with, of course, a small head office to produce the consolidated accounts! Unfortunately, this is rarely the case. Units within the enterprise will trade with each other and use common services – perhaps, for example, occupying a common site – whilst the group's head office will generally raise finance centrally.

The first problem that arises in preparing disaggregated financial statements is defining the segments. If the operating units within the group were completely separate from each other they could be used as the basis for segments, with similar units being aggregated to form a single segment. This would not necessarily be the ideal solution because a single unit might operate in more than one industrial sector so that it would not be possible to find 'single industry' enterprises with which to compare the results of the segment to which that unit was assigned.

In practice, it will not usually be possible to identify units which are completely separate in organizational and economic terms. The Companies Act requirement to disclose information by 'class of business' means that enterprises should in any event base their segment definitions on activity rather than organizational structure although there is likely to be considerable overlap between the two.

Once segmental definitions have been established, the enterprise must decide how to deal with the effects of the organizational and economic interaction between segments. This interaction is likely to take the following forms:

1. Sales between segments.
2. Joint purchasing schemes designed to secure cheaper prices than would be obtained if the segments made their purchases separately.
3. The use of common services, including the sharing of sites, 'in-house' computer bureaux and centralized services such as legal and personnel advice.
4. Loan finance raised centrally and distributed between segments by head office.

In each case there are two decisions to be taken: how the revenues and costs involved are to be spread between the segments, and how the transactions are to be shown in the segmental financial statements. For example, where one segment sells to another, the basis on which those sales are priced will determine how the *group's* profit is distributed between the segments when the goods or services are sold on to a third party. If inter-segmental sales are large enough, head office can influence the level of individual segments' profits by its transfer pricing policy.

In the same way, if a raw material is purchased jointly by two segments to obtain lower prices, the profit of the group will be higher than the combined profit which would be achieved if the two segments were in fact operating as separate enterprises. How is this profit to be distributed between the two segments? There is no non-arbitrary way of splitting the profit – this is one example of what is generally known in financial accounting theory as the 'allocation problem'. Dividing the profit equally, or in proportion to quantities purchased, may appeal to one's sense of fair play but such allocations are no more economically rational than any other.

Inter-segmental transactions can be shown in the financial statements in a variety of ways. Take, for example, inter-segmental sales. Suppose that a two-segment group has sales as shown below and that all internal sales have been sold on to third parties within the period.

	Outside the group £	*To segment A* £	*To segment B* £	*Total* £
Segment A	20,000	—	5,000	25,000
Segment B	30,000	8,000	—	38,000
Total	50,000	8,000	5,000	63,000

The consolidated financial statements of the group will show sales of £50,000. Including inter-segmental sales in the segmental analysis of sales will result in double counting; they can be excluded from the analysis in four ways.

1. By deducting them from the sales of the selling segment, so that a segment's sales represent its sales to third parties. The figures will then be as in the first column of the table above. These tend to understate the total level of activity of the selling segments.
2. By deducting them from the gross figure of total sales of all segments:

	£
Segment A	25,000
Segment B	38,000
	63,000
Less: internal sales	13,000
Total sales	50,000

   This presentation gives a clearer idea of the level of activity of each segment but does not show which segments are interacting and in which direction.
3. By deducting them from the sales of the purchasing segment, so that a segment's sales represent the extent to which sales value has been generated within the segment:

	£
Segment A	17,000
Segment B	33,000
	50,000

   This method gives information about the extent to which sales value is attributable to the activities of the segment, but requires careful interpretation and conceals the extent of segmental interaction.
4. By disclosing all the information in the original table. This represents a much greater degree of disclosure than is common.

In the absence of a UK standard, Reed International was free to select whatever accounting policies it preferred in drawing up its segmental financial statements, subject, of course, to the requirements of the Companies Act and the Stock Exchange and the overriding requirement that the accounts should show a true and fair view.

QUESTIONS

1. List the major matters in respect of which an accounting policy must be selected in drawing up segmental financial statements.
2. Which accounting policies did Reed International use? How were you able to determine which policies were used? Note that the group's statement of accounting policies did not include any policies relating specifically to the segmental report.
3. How would you employ Reed's segmental information in evaluating the performance of the company? Give examples. What additional segmental information would you find useful?
4. How useful would an analyst find the *additional* segmental information given in Reed's operating group reviews? Note that only one review is given as an example in the case material.
5. Do you think your evaluation of Reed would have been different had different accounting policies been used?

FURTHER READING

Emmanuel, C. R. and Gray, S. J. (1977) Segmental disclosures and the segment identification problem, *Accounting and Business Research*, Winter, pp. 37–50.

Institute of Chartered Accountants in England and Wales (1977) *Analysed Reporting*, ICAEW, London.

EXHIBIT 12.1 COMPANIES ACT 1985, SCHEDULE 4, PART III, PARAGRAPH 55

55. Particulars of turnover

1. If in the course of the financial year the company has carried on business of two or more classes that, in the opinion of the directors, differ substantially from each other, there shall be stated in respect of each class (describing it):

   (a) the amount of the turnover attributable to that class; and
   (b) the amount of the profit or loss of the company before taxation which is in the opinion of the directors attributable to that class.

2. If in the course of the financial year the company has supplied markets that, in the opinion of the directors, differ substantially from each other, the amount of the turnover attributable to each such market shall also be stated.

   In this paragraph 'market' means a market delimited by geographical bounds.

3. In analysing for the purposes of this paragraph the source (in terms of business or in terms of market) of turnover or (as the case may be) of profit or loss, the directors of the company shall have regard to the manner in which the company's activities are organized.

4. For the purposes of this paragraph:

   (a) classes of business which, in the opinion of the directors, do not differ substantially from each other shall be treated as one class; and
   (b) markets which, in the opinion of the directors, do not differ substantially from each other shall be treated as one market;

   and any amounts properly attributable to one class of business or (as the case may be) to one market which are not material may be included in the amount stated in respect of another.

5. Where in the opinion of the directors the disclosure of any information required by this paragraph would be seriously prejudicial to the interests of the company, that information need not be disclosed, but the fact that any such information has not been disclosed must be stated.

EXHIBIT 12.2 EXTRACT FROM STOCK EXCHANGE CONTINUING OBLIGATIONS FOR COMPANIES

21. (c) a geographical analysis of both net turnover and contribution to trading results of those trading operations carried on by the company (or group) outside the United Kingdom and the Republic of Ireland;

Explanatory note Transactions within a group should be excluded.

Foreign companies are required to analyse turnover and trading results arising outside their country of incorporation, or the country where the main place of business of the company (or group) is situated.

A broad geographical analysis of net turnover by way of figures or percentages, given by market (not necessarily given country by country), will be acceptable. Where analysis is required, the analysis should be by continent but if 50% of total overseas operation relates to one continent, a further analysis, for example, by country within that continent, will be required. Overseas operations include direct exports and activities carried out otherwise than in the country where the main place of business of the company (or group) is situated.

In respect of trading results an appropriate statement should be included where, for a proper appraisal of the business of the company (or group), holders of listed securities should be aware of significant contributions derived from activities carried out in any one territory. No analysis of the contribution to trading results is required unless the contribution to profit or loss from a specific area is abnormal in nature. Abnormal is defined as substantially out of line with the normal ratio of profit to turnover. For example, if a 40% profit is earned by the group in relation to turnover in one continent, compared with 10% on turnover elsewhere, this fact should be made apparent.

EXHIBIT 12.3 INTERNATIONAL ACCOUNTING STANDARD 14: REPORTING FINANCIAL INFORMATION BY SEGMENT

Definitions

4. The following terms are used in this statement with the meanings specified:

   Industry segments are the distinguishable components of an enterprise each engaged in providing a different product or service, or a different group of related products or services, primarily to customers outside the enterprise.
   Geographical segments are the distinguishable components of an enterprise engaged in operations in individual countries or groups of countries within particular geographical areas as may be determined to be appropriate in an enterprise's particular circumstances.
   Segment revenue is revenue that is directly attributable to a segment, or the relevant portion of revenue that can be allocated on a reasonable basis to a segment, and that is derived from transactions with parties outside the enterprise and from other segments of the same enterprise.
   Segment expense is expense that is directly attributable to a segment or the relevant portion of an expense that can be allocated on a reasonable basis to the segments.

International Accounting Standard 14 comprises paragraphs 20–26 of this statement. The standard should be read in the context of paragraphs 1–19 of this statement and of the preface to Statements of International Accounting Standards.

20. Enterprises whose securities are publicly traded and other economically significant entities including subsidiaries should report the financial information described in paragraphs 21–24 for the industry segments and for the geographical segments which are considered to be significant to the enterprise. When both parent company and consolidated financial statements are presented, segment information need be presented only on the basis of consolidated financial statements.
21. The enterprise should describe the activities of each reported industry segment and indicate the composition of each reported geographical area.
22. For each reported industry and geographical segment, the following financial information should be disclosed:

    (a) sales or other operating revenues, distinguishing between revenue derived from customers outside the enterprise and revenue derived from other segments;
    (b) segment results;

EXHIBIT 12.3 CONTINUED

(c) segment assets employed, expressed either in money amounts or as percentages of the consolidated totals; and
(d) the basis of inter-segment pricing.

23. The enterprise should provide reconciliations between the sum of the information on individual segments and the aggregated information in the financial statements.
24. Changes in identification of segments and changes in accounting practices used in reporting segment information which have a material effect on the segment information should be disclosed. Such disclosure should include a description of the nature of the change, an explanation of the reasons for the change and, where the information is reasonably determinable, the effect of the change.

Transitional provision

25. No comparative figures need be presented in the first period in respect of which this standard is introduced if such information is not readily available.

Effective date

26. This International Accounting Standard becomes operative for financial statements covering periods beginning on or after 1 January 1983 except that, in the interests of uniform application in a particular country, for subsidiaries whose securities are not publicly traded, this standard becomes operative when the requirements expressed in this standard become, in all material respects, accepted practice for economically significant domestic entities in that country.

EXHIBIT 12.4 REED INTERNATIONAL PLC: CONSOLIDATED PROFIT AND LOSS ACCOUNT

Consolidated Profit and Loss Account

for the year ended 31 March 1985

£ million	1985	1984
Turnover note 26	2,115·2	2,043·0
Change in stocks of finished goods and work in progress	6·2	8·7
Own work capitalised	2·2	4·2
Other operating income	12·5	12·6
Raw materials and consumables	(901·2)	(867·6)
Other external charges	(453·8)	(379·4)
Staff costs	(599·0)	(652·7)
Depreciation	(49·9)	(46·1)
Exceptional items	(5·1)	(10·0)
Trading Profit note 4	127·1	112·7
Income from shares in related companies note 12	1·4	2·7
Operating Profit	128·5	115·4
Interest note 5	(21·0)	(19·0)
Profit on Ordinary Activities before Taxation	107·5	96·4
Tax on profit on ordinary activities note 6	(43·3)	(27·7)
Profit on Ordinary Activities after Taxation	64·2	68·7
Outside shareholders' interests	(0·3)	(0·3)
Preference dividends note 7	(0·2)	(0·2)
Profit Attributable to Ordinary Shareholders before Extraordinary Items	63·7	68·2
Extraordinary items note 2	15·0	—
Profit for the Financial year	78·7	68·2
Ordinary dividends paid and proposed note 7	(22·0)	(19·5)
Retained Profit Transferred to Reserves	**56·7**	**48·7**
Earnings per Ordinary Share note 8	**53·6p**	**57·7p**

Reserves		
Opening reserves as previously stated	376·3	327·1
Adjustment for change in accounting policy for intangible assets	(49·7)	(43·7)
As restated	326·6	283·4
Goodwill written off on acquisition	(23·6)	(6·0)
Retained profit for the period	56·7	48·7
Other movements	(4·2)	1·6
Exchange differences	23·0	(1·1)
At 31 March 1985	**378·5**	**326·6**

EXHIBIT 12.5 REED INTERNATIONAL PLC: NOTE 26 ON ACCOUNTS

Notes on the Accounts

£ million

26 **Analysis of Turnover and Profit**

	Turnover		HCA Trading Profit		CCA Trading Profit	
Class of Business	1985	1984	1985	1984	1985	1984
Reed Publishing	523	423	57·2	40·3	49·3	34·6
Consumer Publishing	207	223	11·4	16·0	9·0	13·1
Reed Building Products	194	182	8·9	13·0	2·1	6·5
Paint and DIY	247	183	17·4	11·8	13·0	8·1
Decorative Products	113	105	3·4	3·0	0·7	0·4
Packaging	334	302	18·4	15·0	6·6	7·1
Reed Trading	210	171	9·6	5·6	3·0	2·5
European Paper	196	174	2·3	3·0	(1·8)	1·0
North American Paper	191	176	5·2	6·3	(5·5)	(2·2)
Mirror Group Newspapers	75	277	1·2	5·7	0·6	2·7
Central Items	—	—	(7·9)	(7·0)	(8·2)	(7·2)
Total Turnover/Trading Profit	2,290	2,216	127·1	112·7	68·8	66·6
Inter-Company turnover	(175)	(173)				
Related Companies			1·4	2·7	0·3	1·5
Interest/Gearing			(21·0)	(19·0)	(10·5)	(10·3)
Turnover	**2,115**	**2,043**				
Profit on Ordinary Activities before Taxation			**107·5**	**96·4**	**58·6**	**57·8**
Country of Origin						
UK	1,538	1,616	67·6	71·6	28·8	40·5
Europe	160	158	11·4	6·9	5·8	2·9
USA	344	227	34·2	20·9	27·9	19·2
Canada	213	184	8·8	8·5	1·4	(0·4)
Rest of World	35	31	5·1	4·8	4·9	4·4
Total	**2,290**	**2,216**	**127·1**	**112·7**	**68·8**	**66·6**
Geographical Market						
UK	1,396	1,507				
Europe	249	218				
USA	429	299				
Canada	103	97				
Rest of World	113	95				
Total	**2,290**	**2,216**				
Exports from the UK including Sales to Overseas Subsidiaries						
Reed Publishing	41	36				
Consumer Publishing	21	19				
Reed Building Products	21	20				
Paint and DIY	13	11				
Decorative Products	14	14				
Packaging	8	7				
Reed Trading	8	7				
European Paper	8	7				
Mirror Group Newspapers	1	3				
Total	**135**	**124**				

EXHIBIT 12.6 REED INTERNATIONAL PLC: OPERATING GROUP REVIEW – PAINT AND DIY

Operating Group Reviews

PAINT & DIY

£ million	Sales	Trading Profit	Capital Employed	No. of employees
1985 United Kingdom	126	6·4	47·7	2,800
Overseas	121	11·0	45·3	1,900
1984 United Kingdom	116	5·6	44·1	2,700
Overseas	67	6·2	26·3	1,200

This Operating Group manufactures and markets paint and DIY products in the UK, Continental Europe, North America and Africa. Principal brand names in the UK include Crown Plus Two and Anaglypta, and Polycell.

Trading profits in all the main areas of the group were at or above the previous year's levels. Two acquisitions in the USA during the year contributed £2·9 million to the trading profit of £17·4 million, up from £11·8 million last year.

Crown Paints

Profit in the highly competitive UK decorative market showed some recovery from the disappointing results of the previous year with volumes improving by 11·6%. This recovery was constrained, however, by low margins, particularly in the final quarter when competitive pressures on price were exacerbated by sharp cost rises in certain key raw materials. The premium Crown Plus Two brand was strengthened by the inclusion of Colour Cue, a comprehensive colour co-ordinating system, whilst the launch of the liquid gloss, undercoat and primer range enabled Crown Paints to achieve its highest market share for gloss paint in recent years. The Crown Trade Centres, now numbering 40 throughout the country, continue to develop successfully.

Crown's industrial and protective coatings products made further progress in the area of high performance finishes.

Results from white relief wallcoverings, principally Anaglypta and Supaglypta, were lower than in the previous year due to increased factory costs and a change in sales mix. However, the launch in April 1985 of the new white blown vinyl range will improve the product range and profitability.

Exports of Crown paints reached record levels in the face of continued competition. Overseas, the manufacturing companies in Kenya and Malawi achieved excellent profits, but the results of the Irish company were adversely affected by the depressed economy.

Irlam Inks, manufacturers of printing inks and adhesives, had an extremely disappointing year almost entirely due to an 11 week strike last autumn. This operation is now steadily recovering lost business.

North American Paints

General Paint, despite the continuing depression in Western Canada, produced highly satisfactory results with sales increasing by 5·4%. The opening of three new decorating centres brought the total of such outlets to 42 whilst the installation of an additional modern filling and packaging unit in the Vancouver factory will provide significant operating efficiencies.

Parker Paint of Tacoma, Washington, had another good year during which three new decorating centres were opened bringing the total to nine.

Frazee Industries, a paint and coatings manufacturer of San Diego, California, was acquired in July 1984 for $24 million cash. Sales and profits since acquisition have been very satisfactory. Frazee paint products are distributed through its own 24 stores located in Southern California and Arizona. Additionally, its wallcovering division is a distributor of national wallcovering brands in the 10 Western states. The Frazee market area is one of the fastest growing in the world.

Polycell

Polycell's sales and profit in the UK were maintained at the same high levels as in 1983/84, despite increased competition. The product range was enhanced by the introduction of a renovator for ceramic tiling installations, an improved double glazing system and new painting aid products.

Briton Chadwick, which specialises in paint brushes and rollers, had a good trading year, benefiting from improvements in manufacturing and marketing.

Results from the Continental European Polycell companies were slightly better than last year's despite adverse currency fluctuations and highly competitive markets in Germany and Belgium. These companies improved their product range and extended sales into the car care market.

The predominance of large scale DIY retailers is increasing throughout Europe. The Polycell companies continue to adapt to keep a substantial share of this important market.

In the USA, Roman Adhesives had another very successful year from its sales of wallcovering adhesives. W F Taylor, a specialist floorcovering adhesives manufacturer in Los Angeles, was acquired in December 1984 for $6·5 million cash and has begun to make a useful addition to profits. The profit growth of both companies has been impressive and will benefit in the future from the sharing of product and customer knowledge.

Case 13

Analyses of Shareholdings: British Telecom, Burmah, Laporte, Pearson, Ultramar

OBJECTIVES

1. To examine the information content of voluntary disclosures of shareholdings.
2. To discuss the factors responsible for changes in the pattern of share ownership.

MATERIALS

1. Analyses of shareholdings from the annual reports and accounts of the following quoted companies:

   (a) British Telecommunications plc (Exhibit 13.1);
   (b) Burmah Oil plc (Exhibit 13.2);
   (c) Laporte Industries (Holdings) plc (Exhibit 13.3);
   (d) Pearson plc (Exhibit 13.4);
   (e) Ultramar plc (Exhibit 13.5).

INTRODUCTION

Analyses of shareholdings are a relatively new phenomenon. They represent essentially voluntary disclosures since, to date, there has been no formal attempt to regulate their publication, and it is not surprising, therefore, that a fairly wide variety of reporting treatments has arisen.

There are some formal reporting requirements relating to share ownership and these are contained in the Companies Acts and reporting requirements laid down by the Stock Exchange. Section 235 of the 1985 Companies Act requires the directors' report or the notes to the accounts to show the numbers of shares in the company which are held by each director at the beginning and end of the financial year. The Stock Exchange requires the directors' report to disclose information of any single shareholding which amounts to 5 per cent or more of the company's share capital (*Admission of Securities to Listing,* Section 5, Chapter 2). Any shareholding which is equal to or greater than 5 per cent is referred to by the Stock Exchange as a 'substantial interest'.

Research carried out by the Stock Exchange shows that there has been a continuing decline in the proportion of shares in UK companies held by individuals over the period 1963 to 1981. The proportion held by individuals fell from 54 per cent in 1963 to 28.2 per cent in 1981. In marked contrast to this fall there has been considerable growth by what are known as the institutional investors. These institutional investors comprise mainly the pension funds and insurance companies, but significant amounts are also held by investment trusts and unit trusts. The proportion of share capital held by insurance companies has more than doubled over this eighteen-year period but that held by pension funds has more than quadrupled. What accounts for this fundamental shift in the pattern of share ownership in the UK? It is generally felt that the UK system of taxation of savings has been one of the strongest influences. The particular taxation advantages enjoyed by pension funds and insurance companies during the 1960s and 1970s allowed individuals to benefit from growth in the stock markets and, at the same time, reduce their risk by saving through institutional investors who have the ability to invest the funds at their disposal over a broad range of companies.

Recent developments suggest that these trends are unlikely to continue. Since 1979 the Conservative government has been committed to a programme of wider share ownership, and hopes to reverse the decline of the private investor. It is particularly committed to encouraging ownership by small shareholders, although the term 'small shareholder' has not been defined, and it has sought to achieve this transformation through changes in the tax system which have provided firms with the incentive to introduce share schemes for their employees. Employee stock ownership trusts have been encouraged through taxation incentives provided in the 1980 and 1984 Finance Acts. A number of former nationalized industries have now been privatized, one of the largest privatization issues being the flotation of British Telecom, and these flotations have attracted large numbers of new shareholders. In the case of British Telecom the maximum number of shares for which an individual could subscribe was limited to 800 and the offer price per share was £1.30p.

The new deregulation rules which the Stock Exchange brought into effect in October 1986, coupled with lower transactions costs especially for small investors, are likely eventually to have a profound influence on the pattern of share ownership in the UK. Individuals should find it easier to buy shares. In addition, the government has brought in taxation incentives through the medium of PEPs (personal equity plans) for private investors, and building societies and clearing banks are keen to offer these PEPs to their customers.

Just what effect these changes will have on the future pattern of share ownership, it is difficult to predict. Recent surveys carried out into the changing structure of share ownership have come up with conflicting answers. A 1985 survey by Market Opinion and Research International suggested that less than 10 per cent of adults in the UK were shareholders. However, a survey carried out on behalf of the Treasury in 1986 suggested that 14 per cent of the adult population were shareholders, whilst a later survey on behalf of the Stock Exchange produced a figure of 16 per cent (Wolman 1986). Although these surveys provide an indication of the *numbers* of adults who are shareholders, they do not provide information on how *evenly* these shares are spread among individuals.

Given the level of institutional investment, it is felt by some people that the institutions should become more involved in the management of UK companies and should use their financial expertise to benefit British industry. Although the institutions seem to be reluctant to involve themselves in the day-to-day running of companies, there is some evidence that they may, from time to time, exert influence on management in particular circumstances.

ANALYSIS

So how might shareholders benefit from the publication of analyses of shareholdings? There are several reasons why shareholders could benefit from more information about the dispersion of shareholdings in a company. It is likely, although difficult to prove, that institutional investors may have quite different objectives from individual investors, one possible reason being the different taxation treatment affecting individuals as opposed to institutional investors.

As an example we can take the case of, say, company A which needs to decide what proportion of its profits for the year should be distributed as dividends. If it pays a relatively high dividend, the income of its shareholders will be high. On the other hand, resources retained inside the firm for future investment will be less, and so it is possible that future growth will be less than it would otherwise have been. This means that the company's share price will not increase by as much as company B which tends to retain proportionately more of its profits for future growth. This is obviously a very abstract example since dividend policy is only one of a number of factors which influence share price movements. Moreover, additional investment leading to future growth can be obtained not only through retention of profits but also by fixed-interest loans. Nevertheless, the implications for shareholders in the two companies would be as follows.

A shareholder in company A who pays income tax at the highest marginal rates might be prepared to receive a lower dividend (on which income tax is payable) and gain the benefit of the company's profits by way of increases in the share price (on which capital gains tax at a more favourable rate than income tax would be payable). On the other hand, institutional investors might be indifferent (for tax purposes) between capital gains and income from dividends. In fact there does seem to be some evidence that they are not too happy when a company passes its dividend (i.e. declares no dividend) for a particular year. The reason for this could be that they have regular expenditure commitments (for instance to pay the pensions of their clients) and are therefore interested in receiving a relatively steady stream of dividends from the companies in which they invest.

It is clear that under these conditions institutional investors and private investors would have a conflict of interest. So if it seems likely that pension funds and insurance companies, due to the size of their shareholdings, are in a position to influence management, the company's dividend policy may not accord with what the private investor wants. The Stock Exchange in its survey of share ownership investigated the preferences of different types of investor for buying shares in varying sizes of companies. Insurance companies have a marginal preference for investing in large companies (i.e. companies with a market value between £80 million and £400 million) but otherwise invest fairly evenly over the spread of companies. Personal investors are relatively more concentrated in small companies (under £20 million market value) while pension funds are concentrated in very large (over £400 million market value) and large companies. Therefore, private investors may believe that small and medium-sized companies are less likely to be subject to influence by institutional investors. On the other hand, the fact that the institutions with all their financial expertise are prepared to invest more in very large and large companies may be regarded by some private investors as a 'stamp of approval' for the general management policies of those companies.

A further reason why users of accounts might benefit from more detailed information about share ownership relates to takeover bids. In the period leading up to the public announcement of a takeover bid, there is generally a period during which rumours will cause considerable fluctuations in the share market price of the offeree company (i.e. the company being bid for). Sometimes the offeror company (i.e. the bidding company) will have built up a sizeable stake in the offeree company over a period of time. Therefore, readers of accounts might be able to assess the likelihood of a takeover bid by referring to the compulsory disclosures required by the Stock Exchange relating to substantial interests, and also by analysing (if available) the overall concentration of shareholdings in the company.

A controversial aspect of some recent share issues centres around what have come to be known as 'vendor placings'. Normally a company can increase its share capital by means of a rights issue which means that all existing shareholders are automatically notified of their right to acquire some of the new share capital in proportion to their existing interest in the company. If they do not wish to take up these 'rights' they can normally benefit by selling them. Consequently, an investor's shareholding cannot be diluted without that investor's knowledge and consent. However, rights issues can be a relatively expensive form of raising additional share capital, since it involves notifying all the existing shareholders, and some companies have recently resorted to vendor placings.

Using a vendor placing, a company will allocate all the additional share capital specifically to a few institutional investors. It can be appreciated that if such a placing is based on a price substantially lower than the current share market price, such institutions are indeed in a favourable position. It is quite likely that such vendor placings will become more widely used following the deregulation of the Stock Exchange in October 1986 and the relaxation of the Stock Exchange rules relating to rights issues. Users of accounts, therefore, might wish to monitor the extent to which their control has been eroded through vendor placings, and one means would be by examining the analysis of shareholdings. For instance, by comparing the levels of institutional investment over time a private investor might be able to judge the extent to which the institutions had benefited from vendor placings.

Analyses of shareholdings can be considered in two parts. The first part (for example Pearson, Exhibit 13.4) refers to different types of shareholders, so for the sake of convenience we can refer to it as a 'type' profile. The second part describes the dispersion over different sizes of shareholding, and we can refer to it as a 'dispersion' profile. These are voluntary disclosures and large companies tend to publish them more frequently than smaller companies. Not all companies publish both profiles. Some will publish a type profile but not a dispersion profile and vice versa. Several companies combine the two profiles (as in the case of Laporte, Exhibit 13.3) and one or two companies publish profiles showing the geographical location of the registered shareholder.

A number of difficulties are encountered in trying to make a meaningful assessment of the pattern of share ownership in a company. First, since there is no formal standardization of these statements, the information categories tend to differ between companies. Thus, Burmah has eight categories in its type profile while Pearson has six. It can also be seen that the categories in the dispersion profile vary and the bands are of different width. Thus, the top category for the Ultramar profile (Exhibit 13.5) contains 66.8 per cent of all shareholdings (100,000 shares and over), while the top category for Pearson (Exhibit 13.4) contains 37.7 per cent of all shareholdings (i.e. all holdings over 2 million shares).

Second, we need to consider the question of nominee holdings and beneficial ownership. A beneficial owner is the person or company who is the 'true' owner of the shares and is entitled to all the rights (such as receiving dividends) which attach to those shares. The beneficial owner, for various reasons, may be reluctant to register his or her name on the company's share register but is permitted to employ an agent who acts simply as a 'name' (hence the term nominee) and the shares are registered in the name of the agent. Since we are interested in analysing beneficial ownership rather than nominee holdings we need to look behind the 'names' to find out who the true owners are.

Section 212 of the 1985 Companies Act gives the management of a company the right to request a nominee to disclose the identity of the beneficial owner, and it appears that both Ultramar and Pearson have taken advantage of this provision. Thus, Ultramar (Exhibit 13.5) states that 'all nominee holdings of 100,000 shares and over have been reallocated to the ultimate beneficial owner'. In the case of Burmah (Exhibit 13.2) it does not appear that such a reallocation has been made, since 54.6 per cent of the total stock is in the category 'banks, nominees and trustee companies'. It is thus more difficult to gain an accurate picture of the pattern of ownership for Burmah.

In its 1983 survey of share ownership the Stock Exchange examined a sample of share registers in order to identify the beneficial owners of nominee holdings. It was found that pension funds accounted for 44 per cent, insurance companies 14 per cent and private individuals 8 per cent. Although such percentages need to be treated with some caution they do provide an indication over which beneficial categories the nominees tend to be spread.

Third, in the case of dispersion profiles the basic unit of measurement is the nominal value of a single unit of the company's share capital. In order to compare patterns of shareholdings between companies it is helpful to have access to information about the relevant share market prices.

For the companies whose analyses of shareholdings are reproduced as Exhibits 13.1 to 13.5, the relevant share prices at the date on which the analyses were prepared are as follows.

Company	*Share price (pence)*	*Date*
British Telecom	232	31 May 1986
Burmah	270	31 December 1985
Laporte	345	29 December 1985
Pearson	425	31 December 1985
Ultramar	203	31 December 1985

Finally, it is generally accepted from economic research carried out into patterns of shareholdings in UK companies that shareholding concentration and company size are negatively related. What this means is that the larger company, the more widely dispersed the ownership tends to be. Since smaller companies tend to have more concentrated share ownership, it would be meaningless to make a direct comparison of patterns of ownership between large and small companies unless this factor were taken into account.

QUESTIONS

1. What benefits might a reader of accounts derive from studying an analysis of shareholdings?
2. What difficulties arise in interpreting analyses of shareholdings?

3. What difficulties arise in comparing analyses of shareholdings?
4. How might the difficulties in questions 2 and 3 above be overcome?
5. Why might pension funds prefer to invest in very large and large companies?
6. How would you define a small shareholder?
7. Compare the dispersion profiles for the five companies with regard to ownership by small shareholders and comment on your findings.
8. Compare the type profiles for the five companies with regard to ownership by individuals, pension funds and insurance companies. Comment on these comparisons.
9. Why might the management of a company be interested in identifying the beneficial owners of nominee holdings?

REFERENCES AND FURTHER READING

Stock Exchange (1983) *The Stock Exchange Survey of Share Ownership,* Stock Exchange, London.

Wearing, R. T. (1985) Accounting for share ownership, *Accountancy,* March pp. 169–72.

Wolman, C. (1986) Surge in individual share ownership, *Financial Times,* 26 June.

EXHIBIT 13.1 BRITISH TELECOMMUNICATIONS PLC: ANALYSIS OF SHAREHOLDINGS

Classification of ordinary shareholders at 31 May 1986

	Shareholders	Ordinary shares of 25p each	
	Number of holdings	Number of shares held (millions)	Percentage of total
HM Government	1	2,988	49.8
Trustees of the Employee Share Ownership Scheme (a)	1	53	0.9
Pension funds	504	200	3.3
Insurance companies	374	264	4.4
Banks	1,915	5	0.1
Other corporate bodies (b)	10,320	1,731	28.9
Individuals	1,566,790	758	12.6
Held by Lloyds Bank Plc on behalf of others (c)	1,936	1	
	1,581,841	6,000	100.0

Size of shareholding at 31 May 1986

	Shareholders		Interests in ordinary shares of 25p each	
	Number of holdings	Percentage of total	Number of shares held (millions)	Percentage of total
1–399	457,144	28.9	90	1.5
400–799	760,582	48.1	347	5.8
800–1,599	337,773	21.3	274	4.6
1,600–9,999	23,173	1.5	55	0.9
10,000–99,999	1,855	0.1	59	1.0
100,000–999,999	957	0.1	302	5.0
1,000,000–999,999,999 (b)	356		1,885	31.4
1,000,000,000 and above	1		2,988	49.8
	1,581,841	100.0	6,000	100.0

(a) Under the Employee Share Ownership Scheme, 53 million ordinary shares of the company were held in trust on 31 May 1986 by British Telecom Employee Shares Trustees Limited on behalf of 221,906 participants who were beneficially entitled to the shares under special arrangements made at the time of the Offer for Sale.

(b) Approximately 17 million shares were represented by American Depositary Receipts, which are listed on the New York and Toronto Stock Exchanges. A further 43 million shares, held by Japanese investors, are traded on the Tokyo Stock Exchange. Analyses by classification and size were not available for these holdings.

(c) 849,540 shares on which the final instalment of 40p per ordinary share, due to be paid to HM Government on 9 April 1986, remained outstanding at 31 May 1986.

EXHIBIT 13.2 THE BURMAH OIL PLC: ANALYSIS OF SHAREHOLDINGS

Analysis of ordinary stockholdings

The distribution of ordinary stock at 31 December 1985 was:

£	Number of stockholders	%	Stock held	%
1 – 200	32,380	45·5	3,409,118	2·4
201 – 500	20,274	28·5	7,010,318	4·9
501 – 1,000	9,939	13·9	7,731,234	5·4
1,001 – 5,000	7,533	10·6	15,077,478	10·5
5,001 – 10,000	442	0·6	3,339,665	2·3
10,001 – 25,000	230	0·3	3,787,448	2·6
25,001 – 50,000	112	0·2	4,390,953	3·0
50,001 – 100,000	80	0·1	6,261,134	4·3
100,001 – 150,000	32	0·1	4,094,976	2·8
over 150,000	125	0·2	88,869,902	61·8
Total	71,147	100·0	143,972,226	100·0

The classification of ordinary stockholdings at 31 December 1985 was:

Banks, nominees and trustee companies	1,954	2·7	78,669,501	54·6
Insurance	153	0·2	11,564,842	8·0
Pension funds	46	0·1	3,241,461	2·3
Investment and unit trusts	49	0·1	4,777,717	3·3
Regional and statutory bodies	21	0·1	1,544,434	1·1
Charities and societies	65	0·1	377,739	0·3
Other corporate bodies	876	1·2	7,178,628	5·0
Individuals	67,983	95·5	36,617,904	25·4
Total	71,147	100·0	143,972,226	100·0

EXHIBIT 13.3 LAPORTE INDUSTRIES (HOLDINGS) PLC: ANALYSIS OF SHAREHOLDINGS

Share and Stock Ownership

Analysis at 29th December 1985

	Holdings		Nominal Amount held	
Ordinary shares	**Numbers**	%	**Total £**	%
Individuals—Up to 500 shares	2,570	26.30	353,289	0.52
501 to 2,500 shares	4,537	46.43	2,812,925	4.12
2,501 to 25,000 shares	1,283	13.13	3,153,540	4.61
Over 25,000 shares	40	0.41	3,094,832	4.53
	8,430	86.27	9,414,586	13.78
Nominee companies	953	9.75	32,091,654	46.99
Assurance and insurance companies	145	1.49	8,568,290	12.54
Investment trusts and funds	23	0.24	333,208	0.49
Pension funds and pension trustees	49	0.50	5,953,524	8.72
Other corporate holdings	171	1.75	11,940,281	17.48
	9,771	100.00	68,301,543	100.00
Preference stock				
7½% cumulative preference	138		151,000	
5½% cumulative second preference	143		619,638	
	10,052		69,072,181	

EXHIBIT 13.4 PEARSON PLC: ANALYSIS OF SHAREHOLDINGS

As at 31 December 1985

	HOLDERS	PERCENTAGE	SHARES HELD (000's)	PERCENTAGE
Individuals	13,855	87·8	56,618	28·9
Nominees*	430	2·7	11,059	5·6
Insurance companies	109	0·7	34,309	17·5
Pension funds	231	1·5	54,411	27·8
Banks	337	2·1	1,125	0·6
Other corporate bodies	820	5·2	38,366	19·6
	15,782	100·0	195,888	100·0
1–2,500	12,956	82·0	11,047	5·6
2,501–50,000	2,480	15·7	20,116	10·2
50,001–250,000	235	1·5	26,885	13·7
250,001–1,000,000	73	0·5	34,161	17·5
1,000,001–2,000,000	22	0·2	29,875	15·3
Over 2 million	16	0·1	73,804	37·7
	15,782	100·0	195,888	100·0

*Certain nominee holdings have been re-allocated to other categories according to the beneficial ownership of the shares concerned.

EXHIBIT 13.5 ULTRAMAR PLC: ANALYSIS OF SHAREHOLDINGS

Number of Shares held	Number of Shareholders 31st December 1985	Percentage of total Shares 31st December 1985
1– 999	12,156	2.1
1,000– 4,999	14,524	11.1
5,000– 9,999	2,288	5.5
10,000–49,999	1,503	9.9
50,000–99,999	188	4.6
100,000 and over	315	66.8
	30,974	100.0

Class of Shareholder	Number of Shareholders 31st December 1985	Percentage of total Shares 31st December 1985
Private individuals	26,409	25.2
Insurance companies and banks	963	10.9
Nominee companies	1,601	7.7
Pension funds	206	31.6
Public limited companies	18	6.2
Other corporate bodies	1,777	18.4
	30,974	100.0

The above figures include overseas holdings comprising 10.9 per cent of the total number of issued Shares. The Shares of the Company are listed on the London, Montreal and Toronto Stock Exchanges. In the above analysis by class of Shareholder all nominee holdings of 100,000 Shares and over have been re-allocated to the ultimate beneficial owner.

Case 14
Current Cost Accounting: ICI

OBJECTIVES

1. To investigate the interpretation of current cost accounts.
2. To examine the problems which arise from the 'deregulation' of accounting practice.

MATERIALS

1. Extracts from the annual report and accounts of Imperial Chemical Industries plc for the year ended 31 December 1984:

   (a) profit and loss statement (current cost) (Exhibit 14.1);
   (b) notes relating to the CCA results (Exhibit 14.2);

2. Extracts from the annual report and accounts of Imperial Chemical Industries plc for the year ended 31 December 1985:

   (a) group profit and loss account (Exhibit 14.3);
   (b) balance sheets (Exhibit 14.4);
   (c) CCA information from the report of the directors (Exhibit 14.5).

INTRODUCTION

The first standard to be prepared by the ASC on the subject of accounting for changing prices, PSSAP 7 (the 'P' indicating its provisional – i.e. non-mandatory – status), was issued in 1974 and adopted the current purchasing power approach. This approach fell out of favour after the government's Sandilands Committee, reporting in the following year, recommended current cost accounting. The profession began work on developing methods of reporting in current cost terms; the first exposure draft of the subject, ED 18, was issued in November 1976. This was effectively vetoed by the membership of the Institute of Chartered Accountants in England and Wales who in July 1977 carried a resolution rejecting mandatory use of CCA. The ASC, however, continued its search for an acceptable means of establishing current cost accounting, issuing interim guidelines (again, non-mandatory) in November 1977 and ED 24 in April 1979. SSAP 16, which largely followed the principles of ED 24 and the earlier interim guidance, was finally adopted in March 1980.

In 1985, following increasing resistance to the publication of CCA figures by listed companies – unlisted companies having been reluctant to publish CCA figures all along – the mandatory status of SSAP 16 was withdrawn.

QUESTIONS

1. Indicate how the various adjustments disclosed in the CCA statements for 1984 are arrived at and explain their meaning.
2. Compare the CCA disclosures for 1985 with those for 1984. How useful would a financial analyst find the 1985 figures by comparison with those for 1984?
3. Why might a company be reluctant to prepare and publish CCA statements? Why might a company be prepared to publish CCA information on a voluntary basis?

EXHIBIT 14.1 ICI PLC: CURRENT COST PROFIT AND LOSS STATEMENT 1984

Profit and loss statement (current cost)

For the year ended 31 December 1984

	1984 £m	1983 restated in 1984 £'s £m	1983 £m
Turnover	**9,909**	8,667	8,256
Trading profit			
As in historical cost accounts	**1,063**	728	693
Cost of sales adjustment	**(57)**	(40)	(38)
Monetary working capital adjustment	**(21)**	(22)	(21)
Supplementary depreciation less indexation of government grants	**(156)**	(172)	(164)
Trading profit – current cost	**829**	494	470
Share of profits less losses of related companies and amounts written off investments	**50**	43	41
Profit before financing costs and taxation	**879**	537	511
Interest and other financial items			
As in historical cost accounts	**(100)**	(142)	(135)
Gearing adjustment (note 1)	**63**	68	65
Profit on ordinary activities before taxation	**842**	463	441
Taxation on profit on ordinary activities	**(373)**	(211)	(201)
Attributable to minorities	**(36)**	—	—
Net profit before extraordinary items attributable to parent company	**433**	252	240
Dividends	**186**	154	147
Earnings before extraordinary items per £1 Ordinary Stock	**70.3p**	41.5p	39.5p
Dividends per £1 Ordinary Stock	**30.0p**	25.2p	24.0p
Total depreciation charged, less government grants credited, in current cost accounts	**568**	600	572

Extraordinary items are shown in note 3.

EXHIBIT 14.2 ICI PLC: NOTES RELATING TO THE CCA RESULTS 1984

1 Accounting basis

These statements are prepared on a Current Cost Accounting (CCA) basis in accordance with the principles of Statement of Standard Accounting Practice No. 16. The accounting policies are as adopted in the historical cost accounts, except for modifications required to comply with SSAP 16. The bases for the current cost adjustments are:

a Tangible fixed assets and depreciation:
  i In general, indices of the cost of chemical plant.
  ii Asset lives which are up to one third longer than those applied in the historical cost accounts (see page 33). Based on reviews of asset values and lives which have been undertaken as part of the Group's consideration of the current cost basis of accounting, the Group believes that it is appropriate for CCA purposes to use longer lives from within the range of possible lives.

b Stocks and cost of sales—actual movements in costs, using the averaging method.

c Changes in the requirements for monetary working capital (trading debtors less creditors)—movements in appropriate specific indices.

d Government grants—indices of the cost of chemical plants; grants have been brought into profit over the lives adopted for CCA accounts.

e Appropriate CCA adjustments have been made to the results of related companies.

The gearing adjustment is based on a gearing percentage of 20.0 per cent (1983 22.4 per cent), being the proportion of average non-equity finance to average total investment. For the purpose of calculating the gearing percentage, non-equity finance totalled £1,691m (1983 £1,558m) and comprised loans, short-term borrowings and other non-trading liabilities, less cash and short-term investments. The current cost value of the total investment in the business totalled £8,563m (£7,687m) and comprised tangible fixed assets (less government grants), fixed asset investments and net working capital. In calculating the gearing adjustment, the supplementary depreciation charge is adjusted to make allowance for the difference between historical and CCA asset lives.

To facilitate comparison with 1984 results, 1983 results are shown additionally re-stated in 1984 £'s by applying the movement of 5.0 per cent in the average UK retail price index.

2 Balance sheet at 31 December 1984

	1984 £m	1983 restated in 1984 £'s £m	1983 £m
Fixed assets			
Tangible assets at current cost (gross)	**15,271**	14,653	13,957
Tangible assets net of cumulative depreciation	**6,084**	5,962	5,679
Investments in related and other companies	**805**	794	756
Current assets and liabilities			
Stocks	1,767	1,582	1,507
Debtors, short-term investments and cash	3,113	2,556	2,435
Creditors due within one year	(2,674)	(2,184)	(2,080)
	2,206	1,954	1,862
Total assets less current liabilities	**9,095**	8,710	8,297
Creditors due after more than one year	**1,438**	1,477	1,407
Provisions	**279**	212	202
Grants not yet credited to profit	**609**	668	636
Capital and reserves			
Attributable to parent company			
Share capital	**628**	652	621
Reserves (see below)	**5,440**	5,112	4,870
Attributable to minorities	**701**	589	561
	9,095	8,710	8,297

3 Reserves

	1984 £m	1983 restated in 1984 £'s £m	1983 £m
At beginning of year	**4,870**	4,766	4,540
Adjustment for deferred tax	**(100)**	—	—
Inflation and exchange adjustments	**393**	260	248
Surplus for year			
Before extraordinary items	433	252	240
Extraordinary items	(20)	(61)	(58)
Dividends	(186)	(154)	(147)
	227	37	35
Share premiums	**29**	21	20
Other movements	**21**	28	27
At end of year	**5,440**	5,112	4,870

EXHIBIT 14.3 ICI PLC: GROUP PROFIT AND LOSS ACCOUNT 1985

GROUP PROFIT AND LOSS ACCOUNT

For the year ended 31 December 1985

	Notes	1985 £m	1984 £m
TURNOVER		10,725	9,909
Operating costs	4	(9,917)	(8,990)
Other operating income	4	170	144
TRADING PROFIT (after providing for depreciation 1985 £474m, 1984 £440m)		978	1,063
Share of profits less losses of related companies and amounts written off investments	5	56	71
Net interest payable	6	(122)	(100)
PROFIT ON ORDINARY ACTIVITIES BEFORE TAXATION		912	1,034
Tax on profit on ordinary activities	7	(308)	(373)
PROFIT ON ORDINARY ACTIVITIES AFTER TAXATION		604	661
Attributable to minorities		(52)	(56)
NET PROFIT ATTRIBUTABLE TO PARENT COMPANY		552	605
Extraordinary items	8	(40)	(20)
NET PROFIT FOR THE FINANCIAL YEAR		512	585
Dividends	9	(214)	(186)
PROFIT RETAINED FOR YEAR		298	399
EARNINGS BEFORE EXTRAORDINARY ITEMS PER £1 ORDINARY STOCK	10	86.4p	98.2p

GROUP RESERVES ATTRIBUTABLE TO PARENT COMPANY

	Note	1985 £m	1984 £m
At beginning of year		3,201	2,721
Profit retained for year: Company		98	72
Subsidiaries		219	314
Related companies		(19)	13
		298	399
Amounts taken direct to reserves		(661)	181
Transfer to deferred tax provision		—	(100)
At end of year	11	2,838	3,201

Figures in brackets represent deductions; £m means millions of pounds sterling.

EXHIBIT 14.4 ICI PLC: BALANCE SHEETS 1985

BALANCE SHEETS

At 31 December 1985

		GROUP		COMPANY	
	Notes	1985 £m	1984 £m	1985 £m	1984 £m
ASSETS EMPLOYED					
FIXED ASSETS					
Tangible assets	12	3,533	3,629	1,420	1,306
Investments: Subsidiaries	13			2,538	2,554
Related and other companies	14	287	442	63	78
		3,820	4,071	4,021	3,938
CURRENT ASSETS					
Stocks	15	1,750	1,740	715	690
Debtors	16	1,950	2,102	393	426
Investments and short-term deposits	17	576	865	98	152
Cash	17	221	146	36	18
		4,497	4,853	1,242	1,286
TOTAL ASSETS		8,317	8,924	5,263	5,224
CREDITORS DUE WITHIN ONE YEAR					
Short-term borrowings	18	(511)	(383)	(182)	(103)
Current instalments of loans	21	(131)	(207)	(19)	(19)
Other creditors	19	(1,961)	(2,084)	(1,315)	(1,393)
		(2,603)	(2,674)	(1,516)	(1,515)
NET CURRENT ASSETS (LIABILITIES)		1,894	2,179	(274)	(229)
TOTAL ASSETS LESS CURRENT LIABILITIES		5,714	6,250	3,747	3,709
FINANCED BY					
CREDITORS DUE AFTER MORE THAN ONE YEAR					
Loans	21	1,208	1,311	355	199
Other creditors	19	76	127	535	708
		1,284	1,438	890	907
PROVISIONS FOR LIABILITIES AND CHARGES	20	332	279	64	53
DEFERRED INCOME: Grants not yet credited to profit		198	196	126	129
MINORITY INTERESTS		405	508		
CAPITAL AND RESERVES ATTRIBUTABLE TO PARENT COMPANY					
Called-up share capital	22	657	628	657	628
Reserves: Share premium account		591	415	591	415
Revaluation reserve		89	122	6	6
Other reserves		312	327	239	495
Profit and loss account		1,877	2,294	1,174	1,076
Related companies' reserves		(31)	43		
Total reserves	11	2,838	3,201	2,010	1,992
Total capital and reserves attributable to parent company		3,495	3,829	2,667	2,620
		5,714	6,250	3,747	3,709

EXHIBIT 14.5 ICI PLC: EXTRACT FROM DIRECTORS' REPORT 1985 – CCA INFORMATION

In view of the suspension of the mandatory status of UK Statement of Standard Accounting Practice No. 16, ICI has decided not to publish current cost accounts as part of its annual accounts. The inflation-adjusted profit before tax for 1985 (on the same basis as SSAP 16) was £738 million (1984 in 1985 £s £893 million) compared with £912 million (1984 unadjusted £1,034 million) in the historical cost accounts.

The principal adjustments to 1985 profits were:

	£m
Cost of sales adjustment	–81
Monetary working capital adjustment	+16
Supplementary depreciation	–211
Gearing adjustment	+66

Earnings per share on a current cost basis were 62p (1984 equivalent to 74p in 1985 terms).

Case 15
Off-Balance-Sheet Financing and Window Dressing

OBJECTIVES

1. To investigate the problems of dealing with new forms of commercial activity and financing.
2. To explore the difficulty of interpreting the terms 'true and fair view' and 'substance over form'.

INTRODUCTION

This case examines a variety of *forms* of off-balance-sheet financing and window dressing rather than a specific example of their use.

In December 1985 the Technical Committee of the Institute of Chartered Accountants in England and Wales issued a Technical Release expressing concern at recent trends in the use of off-balance-sheet financing and window dressing. It was suggested that both might mislead users of financial statements and could, in extreme cases, amount to fraud.

The Technical Release defined off-balance-sheet financing as 'the funding or refinancing of a company's operations in such a way that, under legal requirements and existing accounting conventions, some or all of the finance may not be shown on the balance sheet'. Window dressing was defined as involving 'transactions, the purpose of which is to arrange affairs so that the financial statements of the concern give a misleading or unrepresentative impression of its financial position'.

Arrangements under which neither the assets acquired nor the finance used to acquire them appear on an enterprise's balance sheet may be undertaken for a variety of motives. For example, a separate legal entity may be set up to raise the finance and hold the assets so as to isolate the risk involved in the undertaking and, so long as there is no recourse to the assets of the 'sponsoring' enterprise in the event of failure, it might be argued that there is a quite legitimate case for treating the new enterprise as a separate entity. Again, the new undertaking may be set up as a separate entity for tax reasons. On the other hand, it is often suggested that an important motive for the use of off-balance-sheet financing and window dressing is that the interpretation which users of financial statements will place on those statements will be influenced by the appearance or non-appearance of the items concerned. This is particularly likely where ratio analysis is used in the interpretation of statements. Many enterprises are subject to borrowing restrictions which limit the amount they can borrow to a fraction of the equity interest – say 50 per cent. These restrictions are generally imposed by existing borrowers in order to prevent their capital from becoming increasingly risky as the gearing of the enterprise goes up. Because the borrowing restriction is usually based on the numbers in the balance sheet, off-balance-sheet financing effectively avoids the restriction.

The Technical Release suggested that to show a true and fair view, as required by the Companies Acts, it was necessary to account for the arrangements discussed in this case on the basis of their economic substance rather than merely their legal form.

ANALYSIS

Set out below are four examples of arrangements which might fall within the definitions given above of off-balance-sheet financing and window dressing.

1. Company A establishes an 'intermediary' company, B, with a small share capital, 50 per cent of which is held by its bank with A retaining the remainder. B in turn establishes a 'borrowing vehicle', company C, the shares of which are held 50 per cent by A and 50 per cent by B. Under the definition in the Companies Act 1985, C is not a subsidiary of A. However, A can strongly influence, and may be able to control, the activities of C. If the bank objects to any action by C, A can vote in favour of the action with its own shares in C while blocking the use of the other shares by voting against the bank and causing a stalemate in determining the direction in which the votes attaching to B's shares should be cast. C raises a large amount of loan capital from the bank and uses the cash injection to acquire operating assets from A, which it then leases back to A. A uses the proceeds from selling its operating assets partly to repay existing loan capital and partly to acquire additional assets. Since C is not a subsidiary of A, its assets and liabilities would not normally appear in A's consolidated balance sheet. In this instance, however, the only 'external' parties to the various transactions involved are A and the bank; it there were no intermediaries the transactions would usually be

recorded by A as additional bank borrowing used to finance the repayment of existing loans and the acquisition of further assets. If C's assets and liabilities are not included in the group balance sheet, however, it will appear as if the repayment of loans and purchase of new assets were financed by the sale of the original assets.

2. A whisky distiller normally holds its inventory for six years before selling it. A large quantity of two-year-old stock is sold to a finance house at a 'bargain' price with an option for the distiller to buy back the stock in four years' time at a price which represents the price at which the original sale was made plus interest at the current rate on four-year loans. Because the price agreed for the original sale represents a bargain compared to the cost of producing the whisky, it is highly probable that the distiller will find it profitable to exercise the option and resell the whisky in the normal course of business. In the meantime the whisky may well remain on the distiller's premises. If the initial transaction is recorded as a sale in the financial statements of the distiller, the stock and the sum invested by the finance house will not appear on the balance sheet of the distiller.
3. A car distributor receives stock 'on consignment' from the manufacturer and is treated as purchasing an item only when it is sold on to a third party. In effect, the manufacturer is financing the trading stock of the distributor.
4. A subsidiary company within a group issues preference shares which are redeemable at the option of the shareholder and carry a rate of dividend broadly comparable to the rate of interest charged on equivalent loan finance. The shares are issued to a bank. In the subsidiary's own accounts the shares will be shown as part of its share capital, and in the group accounts the shares will normally be included in minority interests rather than in loan capital.

QUESTIONS

1. Explain how each of the above arrangements should be accounted for, giving a numerical example of each and explaining the alternatives available. In deciding how to account for each arrangement, bear in mind the need to show a true and fair view of an enterprise's affairs and the importance of the doctrine of substance over form.
2. What effect would the following considerations, where relevant, have on your answers to question 1?
   (a) whether the new finance was to be used to finance activities substantially different from those undertaken already;
   (b) whether the security given for the new finance extended beyond the assets acquired with it to the other assets of the sponsoring enterprise;
   (c) whether the sponsoring enterprise could continue its operations if the assets included in the arrangement were not in fact available to it.

FURTHER READING

Atchley, K. (1986) Argyll case adopted as rogues' charter, *The Accountant,* 3 March, pp. 12–13.

Atchley, K. (1986) ICAEW guidance has overshot the target, *The Accountant,* 17 March, pp. 12–13.

Rutherford, B. A. (1985) The true and fair view doctrine: a search for explication, *Journal of Business Finance and Accounting,* Winter, pp. 483–94.

Case 16
Interpreting Financial Statements I: Marks and Spencer

OBJECTIVES

1. To investigate the use of ratios in the analysis of financial statements.
2. To consider the problems of interpreting accounting numbers.

MATERIALS

1. Extracts from the annual report and financial statements of Marks and Spencer plc for the year ended 31 March 1985:
   (a) consolidated profit and loss account (Exhibit 16.1);
   (b) balance sheets (Exhibit 16.2);
   (c) notes 1, 2, 3, 11 (part), 12, 15, 16 and 18(a) (Exhibit 16.3).
2. Extracts from the annual report and financial statements of Marks and Spencer plc for the year ended 31 March 1986:
   (a) consolidated profit and loss account (Exhibit 16.4);
   (b) balance sheets (Exhibit 16.5);
   (c) consolidated source and application of funds statement (Exhibit 16.6);
   (d) accounting policies (Exhibit 16.7);
   (e) notes 1, 2, 3, 11 (part), 12, 15 and 16 (Exhibit 16.8);
   (f) five-year record (Exhibit 16.9);
   (g) extract from report of the directors: principal activities (Exhibit 16.10).

INTRODUCTION

This case is rather different in structure from most of those in this book. The questions to be dealt with require an overall evaluation of the enterprise based on the accounting and other financial information provided; they are not directed at individual accounting policies. As much information as possible has been given within the limitations of the space available: an important consideration in answering the questions is the selection of appropriate information from all the data provided.

ANALYSIS

As the cases in this volume demonstrate, the interpretation of individual accounting numbers is far from straightforward. Difficulties of interpretation are compounded when analysts are attempting to reach an overall evaluation of an enterprise on the basis of the total 'package' of information provided in a set of financial statements. An important analytical tool frequently used in interpreting financial statements is ratio analysis; ratios are particularly valuable when used to examine trends through time and to make comparisons between enterprises.

The questions for this case are directed at assessing the performance of Marks and Spencer plc. Ratios will be extremely useful in arriving at an assessment: the questions do *not,* however, provide a list of ratios to be calculated. An important part of answering the questions will be deciding which ratios are relevant. Some assistance is provided in the form of the two checklists below dealing with points to consider in interpreting financial statements: one covers points relating to the tools used to perform the analysis whilst the other is directed at the enterprise under examination. Note that both checklists are concerned with the interpretation of financial statements generally and thus not all the points in the lists will be directly relevant to the case under consideration.

QUESTIONS

1. Draw up a report evaluating the overall performance of Marks and Spencer over the last five years and dealing with profitability, liquidity, asset management and financial structure.
2. What problems did you encounter in using Marks and Spencer's accounts to answer the previous question?
3. What additional information would you have found useful in drawing up your report?
4. On 25 July 1986 the price of a 25p share in Marks and Spencer stood at 197p. Would you have recommended buying Marks and Spencer shares at that price?

FURTHER READING

Morley, M. F. (1984) *Ratio Analysis*, Gee, for the Institute of Chartered Accountants of Scotland, Wokingham, Berkshire.

CHECKLISTS OF POINTS TO CONSIDER IN INTERPRETING FINANCIAL STATEMENTS

Checklist 1 Factors affecting the tools of analysis

General

1. Information imperfect/incomplete as a representation, of the underlying condition of the enterprise.
2. Changes/differences in accounting policies.
3. Impact of inflation and changes in specific prices.
4. Window dressing and other forms of manipulation.
5. Effect of profit and capital being measured as the residue after other items have been accounted for – any errors in measurement elsewhere feed through into profit and capital.
6. Need to relate performance of an individual enterprise to that of the industrial sector and the economy generally.
7. Underlying operational performance of the enterprise will not necessarily be completely reflected in share price.
8. Reporting periods of enterprises may not coincide.
9. Balance sheets reflect only a particular moment in time – values during the period may have been quite different.

Profitability

1. Overall return v. return to shareholders v. return to ordinary shareholders.
2. Date capital invested.
3. Effect of technology v. management efficiency.
4. Expenditure on developing the business expensed rather than capitalized – e.g. staff training.

Liquidity

1. Trade-off between solvency and profitability.
2. Window dressing.

Asset management

1. Information incomplete, e.g. no breakdown of inventory by class of business or of cash v. credit sales.

2. Average of opening and closing balances may not be a good approximation to the actual profile during the year.

Financial structure

1. Balance sheet v. income statement measures.
2. Trade-off between return and safety.

Checklist 2 Factors affecting the enterprise under analysis

The nature of the business

1. Type of business.
2. Changes in the nature of the business through time.
3. Differences between the enterprise's business and 'typical' businesses in the sector.

Management of the business

1. Marketing.
2. Operations (e.g. production, distribution).
3. Personnel.
4. Finance.

Events not reflected in the financial statements

1. Post-balance sheet events.
2. New developments.

The future

1. Company plans and forecasts.
2. Other sources of information.

EXHIBIT 16.1 MARKS AND SPENCER PLC: CONSOLIDATED PROFIT AND LOSS ACCOUNT 1985

CONSOLIDATED PROFIT AND LOSS ACCOUNT

FOR THE YEAR ENDED 31 MARCH 1985

	Notes	**1985 £m**	1984 £m
Turnover	*1*	**3,213·0**	2,868·4
Cost of sales		**2,292·5**	2,059·4
Gross profit		**920·5**	809·0
Other expenses	*2*	**617·1**	529·7
Profit on ordinary activities before taxation	*3*	**303·4**	279·3
Tax on profit on ordinary activities	*4*	**120·3**	111·1
Profit on ordinary activities after taxation		**183·1**	168·2
Minority interests		**2·0**	1·8
Profit for the financial year	5	**181·1**	166·4
Dividends			
Preference shares		**·1**	·1
Ordinary shares:–			
Interim of 1·08p per share		**28·5**	27·0
Final of 2·32p per share		**61·2**	55·3
		89·8	82·4
Undistributed surplus		**91·3**	84·0
Earnings per share	6	**6·9p**	6·3p

EXHIBIT 16.2 MARKS AND SPENCER PLC: BALANCE SHEETS 1985

BALANCE SHEETS
AT 31 MARCH 1985

	Notes	*The Group*		*The Company*	
		1985	1984	**1985**	1984
		£m	£m	**£m**	£m
Fixed assets					
Tangible assets:	9				
Land and buildings		**1,178·4**	1,115·7	**1,121·5**	1,061·4
Fixtures, fittings and equipment		**167·1**	136·8	**147·8**	118·3
Assets in course of construction		**17·3**	33·2	**17·1**	33·0
		1,362·8	1,285·7	**1,286·4**	1,212·7
Investments	*10*	**—**	—	**64·3**	69·2
Net assets of financial activities	*11*	**10·7**	8·0	**—**	—
		1,373·5	1,293·7	**1,350·7**	1,281·9
Current assets					
Stocks		**229·7**	194·1	**185·2**	157·5
Debtors	*12*	**67·4**	61·9	**100·0**	92·1
Investments	*13*	**108·3**	58·4	**102·0**	57·9
Cash at bank and in hand	*14*	**83·8**	73·4	**16·6**	10·5
		489·2	387·8	**403·8**	318·0
Current liabilities					
Creditors: amounts falling due within one year	*15*	**477·3**	396·4	**402·5**	337·1
Net current assets/(liabilities) (excluding financial activities)		**11·9**	(8·6)	**1·3**	(19·1)
Total assets less current liabilities		**1,385·4**	1,285·1	**1,352·0**	1,262·8
Creditors: amounts falling due after more than one year	*16*	**49·3**	49·5	**45·0**	45·0
Net assets		**1,336·1**	1,235·6	**1,307·0**	1,217·8
Capital and reserves					
Called up share capital	*18*	**661·3**	330·5	**661·3**	330·5
Share premium account		**·3**	15·9	**·3**	15·9
Revaluation reserve		**82·9**	391·2	**86·7**	395·6
Profit and loss account		**580·8**	489·2	**558·7**	475·8
Shareholders' funds	*19*	**1,325·3**	1,226·8	**1,307·0**	1,217·8
Minority interests		**10·8**	8·8	**—**	—
Total capital employed		**1,336·1**	1,235·6	**1,307·0**	1,217·8

Approved by the Board
7 May 1985

THE LORD RAYNER
Chairman

W B HOWARD
Deputy Chairman and
Joint Managing Director

EXHIBIT 16.3 MARKS AND SPENCER PLC: EXTRACTS FROM NOTES TO 1985 ACCOUNTS

NOTES TO THE FINANCIAL STATEMENTS

1 Turnover

a Retailing
Turnover represents goods sold to customers outside the Group, less returns and sales taxes.

b Financial activities
Financial activities comprise the operation of the Marks and Spencer Chargecard together with leasing and insurance. Turnover represents the interest and other income attributable to these activities.

In previous years, the amount of income attributable to financial activities was insignificant in the context of the Group financial statements and was included under the category of 'other income'. In preparing the financial statements for the current year, the income in respect of such services for last year has been reclassified.

c Analysis of turnover – by activity and geographical market.

(i) Retailing

	1985 £m	1984 £m
United Kingdom stores	**2,900·2**	2,596·7
Overseas stores:–		
Europe	**80·9**	74·4
Canada	**175·0**	150·2
	255·9	224·6
Export sales outside the Group:–		
Europe	**19·5**	18·3
America	**4·8**	3·2
Africa	**7·6**	5·2
Far East	**6·3**	6·5
	38·2	33·2
	3,194·3	2,854·5
(ii) Financial activities	**18·7**	13·9
	3,213·0	2,868·4

The turnover attributable to financial activities arises wholly within the United Kingdom and the Channel Islands.

EXHIBIT 16.3 CONTINUED

2 Other expenses

	1985 £m	1984 £m
Other expenses comprise:–		
Staff costs (see also note 7)	**382·3**	332·9
Occupancy costs	**79·9**	70·0
Other costs	**88·3**	77·8
including – Auditors' remuneration of £·3 million (last year £·3 million) – Hire of plant and machinery of £2·0 million (last year £1·2 million)		
	550·5	480·7
Repairs, renewals and maintenance of properties, fixtures, fittings and equipment	**29·3**	24·7
Depreciation of tangible fixed assets	**44·3**	34·7
	624·1	540·1
Less: Other income (see below)	**12·8**	15·6
	611·3	524·5
Interest payable (see below)	**5·8**	5·2
	617·1	529·7

The directors consider that the nature of the business is such that the analysis of expenses shown above is more informative than that set out in the Companies Act 1981.

	1985 £m	1984 £m
Other income comprises:–		
Bank and other interest	**1·2**	·7
Profit on sales of tangible fixed assets	**·3**	—
Income from current asset investments:		
listed	**1·1**	·9
unlisted	**7·5**	9·8
Profit on sales of current asset investments	**·6**	1·6
Miscellaneous	**2·1**	2·6
	12·8	15·6
Interest payable comprises:–		
Debenture stocks repayable in more than 5 years	**3·2**	3·2
Bank loans and overdrafts	**2·1**	1·5
Other loans repayable in more than 5 years	**·5**	·5
	5·8	5·2
Included in the trading results of the financial activities:–		
Bank and other interest receivable	**8·0**	6·7
Interest payable on bank loans and overdrafts	**13·0**	10·5
Income from finance leases	**10·4**	6·5
Income from listed current asset investments	**·3**	·3
(Loss)/profit on sales of current asset investments	**(·3)**	·4

EXHIBIT 16.3 CONTINUED

3 Profit on ordinary activities before taxation

	1985 £m	1984 £m
This arises as follows:–		
United Kingdom	**288·7**	265·3
Europe	**7·1**	6·7
Canada	**7·6**	7·3
	303·4	279·3
and can be analysed between:–		
Retailing	**299·4**	275·0
Financial activities	**4·0**	4·3
	303·4	279·3

11 Net assets of financial activities

	1985 £m	1984 £m
Current assets		
Debtors (see **a** below)	**111·0**	131·3
Listed investments – market value £4·0 million (last year £3·4 million)	**4·0**	3·6
Cash at bank and in hand	**4·2**	·2
	119·2	135·1
Current liabilities		
Creditors: amounts falling due within one year (see **b** below)	**72·1**	80·4
Net current assets	**47·1**	54·7
Creditors: amounts falling due after more than one year (see **c** below)	**2·2**	4·1
Provision for liabilities and charges:– Deferred taxation (see **f** on page 34)	**34·2**	42·6
Net assets	**10·7**	8·0

[Notes a to f are not reproduced here.]

EXHIBIT 16.3 CONTINUED

12 Debtors

	The Group 1985 £m	The Group 1984 £m	The Company 1985 £m	The Company 1984 £m
Amounts falling due within one year:–				
Trade debtors	**17·8**	16·0	**16·5**	14·4
Amounts owed by Group companies	**—**	—	**35·9**	33·2
Other debtors	**5·8**	5·3	**5·0**	4·7
Prepayments and accrued income	**11·2**	14·1	**9·6**	12·7
	34·8	35·4	**67·0**	65·0
Amounts falling due after more than one year:–				
Advance corporation tax (see note 17)	**23·3**	18·4	**24·7**	19·9
Other debtors	**9·3**	8·1	**8·3**	7·2
	32·6	26·5	**33·0**	27·1
	67·4	61·9	**100·0**	92·1

Trade debtors include advances to suppliers of £9·4 million (last year £8·7 million) against bills of exchange drawn on the Company in respect of merchandise to be delivered during April and May 1985.

Other debtors include loans to employees, the majority of which are connected with house purchases. Among these are loans made to directors (see note 21(b) and (c)) and a loan to an officer of the Company, the balance of which amounted to £17,480 at 31 March 1985 (last year £19,688).

15 Creditors: amounts falling due within one year:–

	The Group 1985 £m	The Group 1984 £m	The Company 1985 £m	The Company 1984 £m
Bank loans and overdrafts	**91·0**	36·6	**—**	—
Trade creditors	**99·1**	82·1	**90·9**	73·8
Bills of exchange payable	**16·2**	15·2	**16·2**	15·2
Amounts owed to Group companies	**—**	—	**43·8**	·2
Group relief payable in respect of financial activities	**1·9**	25·9	**1·9**	25·9
Taxation	**127·8**	101·9	**121·1**	97·3
Social security and other taxes	**12·1**	13·0	**10·2**	10·6
Other creditors	**49·6**	48·6	**42·6**	43·6
Accruals and deferred income	**18·4**	17·8	**14·6**	15·2
Proposed final dividend	**61·2**	55·3	**61·2**	55·3
	477·3	396·4	**402·5**	337·1

16 Creditors: amounts falling due after more than one year:–

	The Group 1985 £m	The Group 1984 £m	The Company 1985 £m	The Company 1984 £m
Repayable between two and five years:–				
Bank and other loans	**1·7**	1·0	**—**	—
Repayable in five years or more:–				
Debenture loans – secured				
5½% – 1985/1990	**5·0**	5·0	**5·0**	5·0
6½% – 1989/1994	**10·0**	10·0	**10·0**	10·0
7¼% – 1993/1998	**15·0**	15·0	**15·0**	15·0
7¾% – 1995/2000	**15·0**	15·0	**15·0**	15·0
Bank and other loans	**2·6**	3·5	**—**	—
	49·3	49·5	**45·0**	45·0

Debenture loans comprise first mortgage debenture stocks which are secured on certain freehold and leasehold properties of the Company. The Company is entitled to redeem the whole or any part of each stock at par, at any time between the two years shown above.

EXHIBIT 16.3 CONTINUED

18 Called up share capital

a At the Annual General Meeting on 5 July 1984 the authorised capital of the Company was increased by £325 million by the creation of 1,300,000,000 additional ordinary shares of 25p. At the same meeting an ordinary resolution was passed approving a one for one scrip issue which resulted in 1,318,911,755 ordinary shares being issued on 27 July 1984 as a capitalisation of reserves.

EXHIBIT 16.4 MARKS AND SPENCER PLC: CONSOLIDATED PROFIT AND LOSS ACCOUNT 1986

CONSOLIDATED PROFIT AND LOSS ACCOUNT

FOR THE YEAR ENDED 31 MARCH 1986

	Notes	**1986** **£m**	1985 £m
Turnover	*1*	**3,734·8**	3,208·1
Cost of sales		**2,666·5**	2,281·5
Gross profit		**1,068·3**	926·6
Other expenses	*2*	**702·5**	622·5
Profit on ordinary activities before taxation	*3*	**365·8**	304·1
Tax on profit on ordinary activities	*4*	**141·3**	120·6
Profit on ordinary activities after taxation		**224·5**	183·5
Minority interests		**2·1**	2·1
Profit for the financial year	*5*	**222·4**	181·4
Dividends			
Preference shares		**·1**	·1
Ordinary shares:–			
Interim of 1·25p per share		**33·0**	28·5
Final of 2·65p per share		**70·1**	61·2
		103·2	89·8
Undistributed surplus		**119·2**	91·6
Earnings per share	*6*	**8·4p**	6·9p

EXHIBIT 16.5 MARKS AND SPENCER PLC: BALANCE SHEETS 1986

BALANCE SHEETS

AT 31 MARCH 1986

	Notes	The Group 1986 £m	The Group 1985 £m	The Company 1986 £m	The Company 1985 £m
Fixed assets					
Tangible assets:	9				
Land and buildings		**1,243·9**	1,178·4	**1,184·0**	1,121·5
Fixtures, fittings and equipment		**201·4**	167·1	**182·7**	147·8
Assets in course of construction		**16·6**	17·3	**16·4**	17·1
		1,461·9	1,362·8	**1,383·1**	1,286·4
Investments	10	**—**	—	**67·5**	64·3
Net assets of financial activities	11	**18·3**	10·7	**—**	—
		1,480·2	1,373·5	**1,450·6**	1,350·7
Current assets					
Stocks		**235·3**	229·7	**197·7**	185·2
Debtors	12	**102·9**	67·4	**156·5**	100·0
Investments	13	**75·7**	108·3	**63·4**	102·0
Cash at bank and in hand	14	**96·6**	83·8	**19·4**	16·6
		510·5	489·2	**437·0**	403·8
Current liabilities					
Creditors: amounts falling due within one year	15	**481·7**	477·3	**422·0**	402·5
Net current assets (excluding financial activities)		**28·8**	11·9	**15·0**	1·3
Total assets less current liabilities		**1,509·0**	1,385·4	**1,465·6**	1,352·0
Creditors: amounts falling due after more than one year	16	**46·1**	49·3	**45·0**	45·0
Net assets		**1,462·9**	1,336·1	**1,420·6**	1,307·0
Capital and reserves					
Called up share capital	17	**662·7**	661·3	**662·7**	661·3
Share premium account		**5·8**	·3	**5·8**	·3
Revaluation reserve		**84·0**	82·9	**86·7**	86·7
Profit and loss account		**699·9**	580·8	**665·4**	558·7
Shareholders' funds	18	**1,452·4**	1,325·3	**1,420·6**	1,307·0
Minority interests		**10·5**	10·8	**—**	—
Total capital employed		**1,462·9**	1,336·1	**1,420·6**	1,307·0

Approved by the Board
8 May 1986

THE LORD RAYNER
Chairman

W B HOWARD
Deputy Chairman and
Joint Managing Director

EXHIBIT 16.6 MARKS AND SPENCER PLC: CONSOLIDATED STATEMENT OF SOURCE AND APPLICATION OF FUNDS 1986

CONSOLIDATED SOURCE AND APPLICATION OF FUNDS

FOR THE YEAR ENDED 31 MARCH 1986

	1986 £m	1985 £m
Cash and short-term funds at 1 April 1985	101·1	95·2
Source of funds		
Arising from trading		
Profit on ordinary activities before taxation	365·8	304·1
Depreciation	52·7	44·7
Sales of fixed assets	5·5	2·4
	424·0	351·2
From other sources		
Shares issued under employees' share schemes	6·9	6·4
	532·0	452·8
Application of funds		
Payment of dividends	94·3	83·9
Payment of taxation	119·7	94·1
Purchase of fixed assets	158·9	121·8
Miscellaneous	(0·2)	2·3
Increase in net assets of financial activities excluding taxation (see below)	5·9	7·9
	378·6	310·0
Increase/(decrease) in working capital		
Stock	5·6	35·6
Debtors	47·5	·6
Creditors under one year (excluding taxation and dividends)	(34·6)	(18·7)
Group relief payable to financial activities	(5·0)	24·0
Creditors over one year	3·2	·2
	16·7	41·7
	395·3	351·7
Cash and short-term funds at 31 March 1986	136·7	101·1

Cash and short-term funds comprise cash at bank and in hand and current asset investments less bank loans and overdrafts.

	1986 £m	1985 £m
Increase in net assets of financial activities		
Purchase of assets for finance leasing	·1	28·6
Capital repayments on leases	(20·6)	(13·9)
	(20·5)	14·7
Increase in fixed assets	4·0	—
Increase in trade debtors	84·2	4·2
Increase/(decrease) in group relief receivable	5·0	(24·0)
(Increase)/decrease in bank loans and overdrafts	(73·1)	9·4
Increase in other working capital	6·3	3·6
Net movement	5·9	7·9

EXHIBIT 16.7 MARKS AND SPENCER PLC: ACCOUNTING POLICIES 1986

ACCOUNTING POLICIES

Basis of accounting
The financial statements are drawn up on the historical cost basis of accounting, modified to include the valuation of the United Kingdom properties at 31 March 1982.

Basis of consolidation
The Group financial statements incorporate the financial statements of:–

(i) The retailing activities of Marks and Spencer p.l.c. and its wholly-owned subsidiaries to 31 March.

(ii) The partly-owned Canadian subsidiary to 31 January. The directors consider that if the Canadian subsidiary prepared financial statements to 31 March, it would unduly delay the presentation of consolidated financial statements to the members of Marks and Spencer p.l.c.

(iii) The financial activities of the Group's wholly-owned subsidiaries to 31 March. In order to reflect the different nature of the business of the financial activities and so present fairly the Group's state of affairs, the assets and liabilities of such activities are shown as a net investment in the Group balance sheet and are analysed separately in note 11 on pages 32 and 33.

Deferred taxation
Deferred taxation is provided on the liability method, to the extent that it is probable that a liability will crystallise. It is provided on the excess of capital allowances over depreciation in respect of assets leased to third parties and on certain items of income and expenditure included in the profit and loss account in different years from those in which they are assessed for taxation purposes.

Depreciation
Depreciation is provided to write off the cost or valuation of tangible fixed assets by equal annual instalments at the following rates:–

Freehold and leasehold land over 99 years – Nil
Leasehold land 50–99 years – 1%
Freehold and leasehold buildings over 50 years – 1%
Leasehold land and buildings under 50 years – Over the remaining period of the lease
Fixtures, fittings and equipment – 10% or 20% according to the estimated life of the asset.

Foreign currencies
The trading results of overseas subsidiaries have been translated using average rates of exchange ruling during the financial year. This represents a change of accounting policy from that previously adopted. Where relevant, last year's figures have been restated. This change in policy does not affect the balance on the profit and loss account and accordingly a restatement of reserves in accordance with Statement of Standard Accounting Practice No 6 is not required.

The balance sheets of overseas subsidiaries have been translated into sterling at the rates of exchange ruling at 31 March. Exchange differences arising between the translation into sterling of the net assets of these subsidiaries at rates ruling at the beginning and end of the year are dealt with through reserves.

The cost of the Company's investment in overseas subsidiaries is translated at the rate ruling at the date of investment.

All other foreign currency assets and liabilities of the Company and its United Kingdom subsidiaries are translated into sterling at the rate ruling at 31 March, except in those instances where forward cover has been arranged in which case this forward rate is used. These exchange differences are dealt with through the profit and loss account.

Transactions during the year between the Company and its subsidiaries, customers and suppliers are translated into sterling at the rate of exchange ruling on the date of the transaction. All profits and losses on exchange realised during the year are dealt with through the profit and loss account.

Pension contributions
The Group operates pension schemes for the benefit of all its employees. The funds of the schemes are administered by Trustees and are separate from the Group. Independent actuaries complete valuations at least every 3 years and, in accordance with their recommendations, annual contributions are paid to the schemes so as to secure the benefits set out in the rules and the periodic augmentation of current pensions. The cost of these is charged against profits when the contributions arise.

Repairs and renewals
Expenditure on repairs, renewals and minor items of equipment is written off in the year in which it is incurred.

Stocks
Stocks which consist of goods for resale are valued at the lower of cost and net realisable value. Cost is computed by deducting the gross profit margin from the selling value of stock. When computing net realisable value an allowance is made for future markdowns.

Leases
For finance leases where the Group is the lessor, gross earnings are allocated to accounting periods such that the profit after tax represents a constant rate of return on the net cash investment in the lease during the period of the lease.

The net investment in finance leases which represents total lease payments receivable net of finance charges allocated to future periods, has been included under debtors in the net assets of financial activities.

Trading results in the United Kingdom
The trading results in the United Kingdom include transactions at stores up to and including the nearest Saturday to 31 March. All other transactions are included up to 31 March in each year.

EXHIBIT 16.8 MARKS AND SPENCER PLC: EXTRACTS FROM NOTES TO 1986 ACCOUNTS

NOTES TO THE FINANCIAL STATEMENTS

1 Turnover

a Retailing
Turnover represents goods sold to customers outside the Group, less returns and sales taxes.

b Financial activities
Financial activities comprise the operation of the Marks and Spencer Chargecard together with leasing and insurance. Turnover represents the interest and other income attributable to these activities.

c Analysis of turnover – by activity and geographical market.

(i) Retailing	1986 £m	1985 £m
United Kingdom stores	3,395·4	2,900·2
Overseas stores:–		
Europe	94·1	82·4
Canada	181·5	175·6
	275·6	258·0
Export sales outside the Group:–		
Europe	25·6	19·5
America	6·4	4·8
Africa	4·8	7·6
Far East	8·0	6·3
	44·8	38·2
	3,715·8	3,196·4
(ii) Financial activities	19·0	11·7
	3,734·8	3,208·1

The turnover attributable to financial activities arises wholly within the United Kingdom and the Channel Islands.

£7·0 million of last year's financial activities turnover has been reclassified in order to more correctly reflect the parent company's treasury activities. Amounts invested and borrowed by the parent company through its finance subsidiary have been included as interest receivable and interest payable.

EXHIBIT 16.8 CONTINUED

2 **Other expenses**

	1986 £m	1985 £m
Other expenses comprise:–		
Staff costs (see also note 7)	**421·7**	384·8
Occupancy costs	**89·1**	81·6
including – Rentals under operating leases of £28·2 million (last year £26·1 million)		
Other costs	**120·6**	89·0
including – Auditors' remuneration of £·4 million (last year £·3 million)		
– Hire of plant and machinery of £2·5 million (last year £2·0 million)		
	631·4	555·4
Repairs, renewals and maintenance of properties, fixtures, fittings and equipment	**33·6**	29·4
Depreciation of tangible fixed assets	**53·0**	44·7
	718·0	629·5
Less: Other income (see below)	**26·6**	19·8
	691·4	609·7
Interest payable (see below)	**11·1**	12·8
	702·5	622·5

The directors consider that the nature of the business is such that the analysis of expenses shown above is more informative than that set out in the formats in the Companies Act 1985.

	1986 £m	1985 £m
Other income comprises:–		
Bank and other interest	**12·8**	8·2
Profit on sales of tangible fixed assets	**·8**	·3
Income from current asset investments:		
listed	**1·9**	1·6
unlisted	**7·6**	7·5
Profit on sales of current asset investments	**1·3**	·1
Miscellaneous	**2·2**	2·1
	26·6	19·8

	1986 £m	1985 £m
Interest payable comprises:–		
Debenture stocks – repayable between 2 and 5 years	**·3**	—
Debenture stocks – repayable in more than 5 years	**2·9**	3·2
Bank loans and overdrafts	**7·9**	9·1
Other loans repayable in more than 5 years	**—**	·5
	11·1	12·8

	1986 £m	1985 £m
Included as turnover or cost of sales in the trading results of the financial activities:–		
Bank and other interest receivable	**9·0**	1·0
Income from finance leases	**8·4**	10·4
Income from listed current asset investments	**·4**	·3
Profit/(loss) on sales of current asset investments	**·1**	(·3)
Interest payable on bank loans and overdrafts	**12·3**	6·1

EXHIBIT 16.8 CONTINUED

3 Profit on ordinary activities before taxation

	1986 £m	1985 £m
This arises as follows:–		
United Kingdom	**346·3**	288·7
Europe	**10·6**	7·2
Canada	**8·9**	8·2
	365·8	304·1
and can be analysed between:–		
Retailing	**370·9**	300·1
Financial activities	**(5·1)**	4·0
	365·8	304·1

11 Net assets of financial activities

	1986 £m	1985 £m
Fixed assets		
Land and buildings	**·4**	—
Assets in course of construction	**·3**	—
Fixtures, fittings and equipment	**3·3**	—
	4·0	—
Current assets		
Debtors	**184·5**	111·0
Listed investments – market value £5·1 million (last year £4·0 million)	**4·6**	4·0
Cash at bank and in hand	**2·2**	4·2
	191·3	119·2
Current liabilities		
Creditors: amounts falling due within one year	**145·0**	72·1
Net current assets	**46·3**	47·1
Total assets less current liabilities	**50·3**	47·1
Creditors: amounts falling due after more than one year	**5·0**	2·2
Provision for liabilities and charges:–		
Deferred taxation	**27·0**	34·2
Net assets	**18·3**	10·7

EXHIBIT 16.8 CONTINUED

12 Debtors

	The Group 1986 £m	*The Group* 1985 £m	*The Company* 1986 £m	*The Company* 1985 £m
Amounts falling due within one year:–				
Trade debtors	**18·6**	17·8	**17·4**	16·5
Amounts owed by Group companies	**—**	—	**58·2**	35·9
Other debtors	**8·8**	5·8	**6·5**	5·0
Prepayments and accrued income	**53·6**	11·2	**51·8**	9·6
	81·0	34·8	**133·9**	67·0
Amounts falling due after more than one year:–				
Advance corporation tax recoverable on the proposed final dividend	**28·6**	26·2	**28·6**	26·2
Deferred taxation provision arising on short-term timing differences	**(17·3)**	(2·9)	**(15·8)**	(1·5)
	11·3	23·3	**12·8**	24·7
Other debtors	**10·6**	9·3	**9·8**	8·3
	21·9	32·6	**22·6**	33·0
	102·9	67·4	**156·5**	100·0

Trade debtors include advances to suppliers of £9·5 million (last year £9·4 million) against bills of exchange drawn on the Company in respect of merchandise to be delivered during April and May 1986.

Other debtors include loans to employees, the majority of which are connected with house purchases. Among these are loans made to directors (see note 20(a) and (b)) and a loan to an officer of the Company, the balance of which amounted to £15,272 at 31 March 1986 (last year £17,480).

As a consequence of a change in the funding arrangements of the Pension Scheme prepayments and accrued income include £44·1 million in respect of 1986/87.

The increase in the Group's provision for deferred taxation of £14·4 million (last year £2·4 million decrease) is represented by a transfer from (last year transfer to) the profit and loss account.

EXHIBIT 16.8 CONTINUED

15 Creditors: amounts falling due within one year:–

	The Group 1986	The Group 1985	The Company 1986	The Company 1985
	£m	£m	**£m**	£m
Bank loans and overdrafts	**35·6**	91·0	**—**	—
Trade creditors	**107·8**	99·1	**100·3**	90·9
Bills of exchange payable	**18·4**	16·2	**18·4**	16·2
Amounts owed to Group companies	**—**	—	**·2**	43·8
Group relief payable in respect of financial activities	**6·9**	1·9	**6·9**	1·9
Taxation	**139·1**	127·8	**133·3**	121·1
Social security and other taxes	**16·0**	12·1	**13·8**	10·2
Other creditors	**55·0**	49·6	**51·5**	42·6
Accruals and deferred income	**32·8**	18·4	**27·5**	14·6
Proposed final dividend	**70·1**	61·2	**70·1**	61·2
	481·7	477·3	**422·0**	402·5

16 Creditors: amounts falling due after more than one year:–

	The Group 1986	The Group 1985	The Company 1986	The Company 1985
Repayable between two and five years:–				
Debenture loan – secured				
5½% – 1985/1990	**5·0**	—	**5·0**	—
Bank and other loans	**1·1**	1·7	**—**	—
Repayable in five years or more:–				
Debenture loans – secured				
5½% – 1985/1990	**—**	5·0	**—**	5·0
6½% – 1989/1994	**10·0**	10·0	**10·0**	10·0
7¼% – 1993/1998	**15·0**	15·0	**15·0**	15·0
7¾% – 1995/2000	**15·0**	15·0	**15·0**	15·0
Bank and other loans	**—**	2·6	**—**	—
	46·1	49·3	**45·0**	45·0

Debenture loans comprise first mortgage debenture stocks which are secured on certain freehold and leasehold properties of the Company. The Company is entitled to redeem the whole or any part of each stock at par, at any time between the two years shown above.

EXHIBIT 16.9 MARKS AND SPENCER PLC: FIVE-YEAR RECORD 1986

Year ended 31 March *(1982 – 53 weeks)*	**1986** **£m**	1985 £m	1984* £m	1983* £m	1982* £m
Turnover (excluding sales taxes)	**3,734·8**	3,208·1	2,862·5	2,509·9	2,204·9
Profit on ordinary activities before taxation	**365·8**	304·1	279·3	239·3	222·1
Tax on profit on ordinary activities	**141·3**	120·6	111·1	102·5	100·3
Profit for the financial year	**222·4**	181·4	166·4	135·2	120·7
Shareholders' funds	**1,452·4**	1,325·3	1,226·8	1,140·0	1,063·7
Funds retained in the business (including depreciation)	**172·2**	136·3	118·7	96·2	81·8
Earnings per share (as adjusted for scrip issue in July 1984)	**8·4p**	6·9p	6·3p	5·15p	4·6p
Dividend on ordinary shares (as adjusted for scrip issue in July 1984)	**3·9p**	3·4p	3·125p	2·55p	2·3p

* Figures have not been restated to show translation using average rates of exchange.

EXHIBIT 16.10 MARKS AND SPENCER PLC: EXTRACT FROM DIRECTORS' REPORT 1986

REPORT OF THE DIRECTORS

Principal activities

Retailing

The Group sells clothing, household goods and foods under the St. Michael trade mark in its chain of stores in the United Kingdom, France, Belgium and Ireland. It also sells a range of St. Michael merchandise and other consumer goods through a chain of stores in Canada. St. Michael merchandise is also sold for export.

Financial activities

These comprise the operation of the Marks and Spencer Chargecard together with leasing and insurance activities.

Case 17
Interpreting Financial Statements II: Wm Morrison Supermarkets, Tarmac

OBJECTIVES

1. To compare the performance of two companies which operate in different industrial sectors.
2. To gain an insight into the nature of a company's operations through the use of ratio analysis.
3. To examine the limitations of financial ratios.

MATERIALS

1. Extracts from the annual report of Tarmac plc for the year ended 31 December 1985:

   (a) group profit and loss account (Exhibit 17.1);
   (b) group balance sheet (Exhibit 17.2);
   (c) notes 14 and 15 (Exhibit 17.3).

2. Extracts from the report and financial statements of Wm Morrison Supermarkets plc for the year ended 1 February 1986:

   (a) consolidated profit and loss account (Exhibit 17.4);
   (b) consolidated balance sheet (Exhibit 17.5);
   (c) notes 14, 15 and 16 (Exhibit 17.6).

INTRODUCTION

This case aims to illustrate the problems which can arise in attempting intercompany comparisons by referring to the annual accounts of two companies operating in different industrial sectors. It also aims to use financial ratios to highlight the different nature of these two companies' activities. Wm Morrison Supermarkets is essentially a trading organization since its principal activity is the retail distribution of goods through supermarkets. A relatively small part of its activities is concerned with the manufacture of fresh food products. Tarmac, on the other hand, is an industrial group which undertakes a number of manufacturing activities including quarrying, manufacturing building products, construction and housing. Intercompany comparisons can be useful in evaluating performance although the problems are considerably reduced if the companies operate in the same industrial sector.

ANALYSIS

Inter-temporal comparisons are considerably easier to make than intercompany comparisons. Although accounting policies may differ between companies, they tend to be applied consistently through time in accordance with SSAP 2 where consistency is referred to as one of the four fundamental accounting concepts. For example, given the different nature of their operations, it is not surprising that the two companies adopt different depreciation rates. Tarmac assumes lives for plant, machinery and vehicles which vary between two and twenty-five years. Wm Morrison Supermarkets, however, writes off such fixed assets over periods between four and five years. In both cases the rates are consistently applied. It could be argued that, provided the respective periods represent genuine estimates of expected asset lives, financial ratios which incorporate these values are comparable.

We should be aware that any substantial changes in the type of operation and/or the level of operational activity may distort the picture provided by a ratio. For example, a large increase in fixed assets in one particular year could dilute the overall profitability of a firm if its impact on profits were not fully felt until a later period.

It should be stressed that performance evaluation through financial ratios requires a great deal of care. Ratios by themselves rarely offer conclusive proof about managerial performance. A firm might appear to be performing poorly compared with a previous period but, if a recession is taking place, in the context of the industry and the economy as a whole, it could be performing relatively well. However, a thoughtful approach to ratio analysis should help to build up an overall picture of performance which may help to suggest areas where improvements could be made.

A number of points need to be remembered when using financial ratios. Many ratios compare 'stocks' (in the sense of items of value at a point in time) with 'flows' (for example continuous streams of revenues or expenses). Should we relate the 'flow' to the 'stock' at the beginning, middle or end of the period or should we take an average? There is no straightforward answer. Often a pragmatic approach will have to be taken (for example using year-end values) if access to previous years' accounts is not possible.

Many companies use different financial year-ends. The year-end for Wm Morrison Supermarkets in 1986 was 1 February which was a Saturday. This choice for ending the financial year (strictly speaking fifty-two weeks) is reasonable since problems of stock counting and valuation are reduced. The stock on the company's premises at the end of a Saturday's trading will be relatively low. It does mean that some ratios, such as stock turnover ratios, may not be representative of the year as a whole and may not be realistic when compared with another trading organization which chooses a different year-end.

The distinctive nature of the two companies' operations needs to be remembered when calculating ratios such as debtor turnover. Since the bulk of the sales of Wm Morrison Supermarkets can be assumed to be on a cash basis, a ratio such as debtor turnover would only be useful if credit sales could be separately identified. This is not generally possible. In addition, measures such as the current ratio or liquid ratio for a supermarket group may appear to be relatively low. Once again, it is in the nature of their operations that nearly all sales are on a cash basis and, therefore, straightforward comparisons between different types of organization may be misleading.

QUESTIONS

1. Calculate financial ratios for Tarmac (1984 and 1985) and Wm Morrison Supermarkets (1985 and 1986) relating to profitability, liquidity, asset management and financial structure. (It should be noted that the called up share capital of Tarmac includes some preference shares, but since they amount to just over 0.1 per cent of the ordinary share capital they can be assumed to be negligible. The called up share capital of Wm Morrison Supermarkets is made up entirely of ordinary shares.)
2. Comment on the picture of the two companies presented by the ratios you have calculated. To what extent are the changes you identify within or outside the control of management?
3. Comment on the inherent limitations of each of the ratios which you have calculated.

EXHIBIT 17.1 TARMAC PLC: GROUP PROFIT AND LOSS ACCOUNT

GROUP PROFIT AND LOSS ACCOUNT

for the year ended 31st December, 1985	Note	1985 £m	1984 £m
Turnover		1,570.6	1,321.2
Deduct turnover of related companies		34.5	44.6
		1,536.1	1,276.6
Cost of sales		1,167.7	965.8
Gross profit		368.4	310.8
Other expenses	1	211.7	187.0
Operating profit		156.7	123.8
Interest payable	2	21.5	14.2
Profit on ordinary activities before taxation	3	135.2	109.6
Taxation on profit on ordinary activities	4	47.6	38.2
Profit on ordinary activities after taxation		87.6	71.4
Minority interests		0.4	0.8
Profit before extraordinary item		87.2	70.6
Extraordinary item	6	5.1	(4.8)
Profit attributable to Tarmac PLC	7	92.3	65.8
Dividends	8	29.1	24.0
Retained profit of the year		63.2	41.8
Earnings per ordinary share before extraordinary item	9	28.2p	25.8p

EXHIBIT 17.2 TARMAC PLC: GROUP BALANCE SHEET

GROUP BALANCE SHEET

at 31st December, 1985			1985		1984
	Note	£m	£m	£m	£m
Assets employed					
Fixed assets					
Tangible assets	10	456.7		430.7	
Investments	11	3.8		9.8	
			460.5		440.5
Current assets					
Stocks	12	310.1		234.9	
Long term contract work in progress	13	18.6		20.7	
Debtors	14	228.4		213.1	
Cash		10.2		11.8	
		567.3		480.5	
Current liabilities					
Creditors: amounts falling due within one year					
Short term borrowings	15	15.3		41.0	
Other creditors	15	385.9		369.5	
		401.2		410.5	
Net current assets			166.1		70.0
Total assets less current liabilities			626.6		510.5
Creditors: amounts falling due after more than one year					
Term loans	16	121.0		102.4	
Deferred liabilities	17	44.0		32.7	
			165.0		135.1
Provisions for liabilities	18		32.7		37.7
Net assets			428.9		337.7
Financed by					
Capital and reserves					
Called up share capital	21		154.9		77.2
Share premium account	22	15.0		90.4	
Revaluation reserve	22	82.5		45.2	
Profit and loss account	22	174.3		120.8	
			271.8		256.4
Shareholders' funds			426.7		333.6
Minority interests			2.2		4.1
Total capital employed			428.9		337.7

Sir Eric Pountain *Chairman*

G. D. W. Odgers *Group Managing Director*

The accounts were approved by the board of directors on 29th April, 1986

EXHIBIT 17.3 TARMAC PLC: EXTRACTS FROM NOTES ON ACCOUNTS

14. Debtors

	Group		Company	
	1985	1984	1985	1984
	£m	£m	£m	£m
Trade debtors	179.9	175.8	—	—
Amounts owed by group companies	—	—	21.0	11.4
Amounts owed by related companies	15.2	9.1	—	—
Prepayments and accrued income	11.0	8.6	0.4	0.6
Other debtors	22.3	19.6	0.3	0.2
	228.4	213.1	21.7	12.2
Included in the above are debtors falling due after more than one year				
Trade debtors	0.1	0.6		
Other debtors	1.0	1.4		

Interest free loans to employees who have subsequently been appointed directors of the company amounting to £23,450 (1984, £23,450) are included in other debtors. The individual loans outstanding at 31st December, 1985 were: D. T. Carr, £10,000, S. F. Pickstock, £8,750 and P. B. Woodman, £4,700.
These loans have all subsisted throughout the year. Also included in other debtors is a loan of £5,450 (1984, £5,450) to an officer of the company.

15. Creditors

	Group		Company	
Amounts falling due within one year	1985	1984	1985	1984
	£m	£m	£m	£m
Short term borrowings				
6¾ per cent Debenture stock 1986/91 redeemable at par	0.2	—	0.2	—
Current instalments due on term loans	0.5	0.1	—	—
Bank loans and overdrafts	14.6	40.9	4.7	23.8
	15.3	41.0	4.9	23.8
Other creditors				
Payments received on account	9.9	12.5	—	—
Trade creditors	214.5	197.2	0.2	0.2
Amounts owed to group companies	—	—	0.4	0.5
Amounts owed to related companies	13.5	14.3	1.4	1.1
Corporation tax	30.7	24.9	3.0	1.2
Other taxation and social security costs	29.3	31.1	9.6	9.3
Proposed dividends	22.3	18.6	22.3	18.6
Accruals	36.7	35.1	2.2	1.3
Other creditors	29.0	35.8	9.8	13.7
	385.9	369.5	48.9	45.9
	401.2	410.5	53.8	69.7

EXHIBIT 17.4 WM MORRISON SUPERMARKETS PLC: CONSOLIDATED PROFIT AND LOSS ACCOUNT

Wm Morrison Supermarkets PLC

Consolidated profit and loss account

52 weeks ended 1 February 1986

	Notes	1986		1985	
		£000's	£000's	£000's	£000's
Turnover			367,987		336,235
Change in stocks			4,566		2,860
Other operating income	1		1,380		1,164
			373,933		340,259
Raw materials and consumables		313,678		288,944	
Staff costs	3	26,561		23,675	
Depreciation of tangible fixed assets		3,878		3,155	
Other operating charges		13,967	358,084	11,595	327,369
Operating profit	4		15,849		12,890
Share in profit of associated company			71		64
Other investment income	5		—		1
Net interest receivable/(payable)	6		568		(608)
Profit on ordinary activities before taxation and profit sharing			16,488		12,347
Profit sharing			787		614
Profit on ordinary activities before taxation			15,701		11,733
Taxation	7		6,507		5,346
Profit for the financial year	8		9,194		6,387
Dividends	9		1,251		1,016
Profit retained	20		7,943		5,371
Earnings per share	10		9·94p		6·92p

EXHIBIT 17.5 WM MORRISON SUPERMARKETS PLC: CONSOLIDATED BALANCE SHEET

Wm Morrison Supermarkets PLC

Consolidated balance sheet
at 1 February 1986

	Notes	1986		1985	
		£000's	£000's	£000's	£000's
Fixed assets					
Tangible	11a	71,795		60,627	
Investments	12a	375		333	
Loan redemption fund	13	103	72,273	96	61,056
Current assets					
Stocks		26,668		22,102	
Debtors	14	2,652		1,966	
Cash at bank and in hand		1,000		1,114	
		30,320		25,182	
Creditors—amounts falling due within one year	15	53,002		44,545	
Net current liabilities			(22,682)		(19,363)
Total assets less current liabilities			49,591		41,693
Creditors—amounts falling due after more than one year	16		(200)		(200)
Provision for liabilities and charges	17		(1,721)		(2,007)
			47,670		39,486
Capital and reserves					
Called up share capital	18		9,269		4,617
Share premium account	18		186		29
Profit and loss account	19		38,215		34,840
			47,670		39,486

K D MORRISON } *Directors*
R W STOTT

3 April 1986

EXHIBIT 17.6 WM MORRISON SUPERMARKETS PLC: EXTRACTS FROM NOTES ON ACCOUNTS

14 Debtors

	Group 1986 £000's	Group 1985 £000's	Holding company 1986 £000's	Holding company 1985 £000's
Due within one year				
Trade debtors	1,907	1,280	1,892	1,246
Amounts owed by subsidiary companies	—	—	—	651
Payments in advance	745	686	731	674
	2,652	1,966	2,623	2,571

15 Creditors—amounts falling due within one year

	Group 1986 £000's	Group 1985 £000's	Holding company 1986 £000's	Holding company 1985 £000's
Bank loans and overdrafts	9,793	8,846	8,827	7,878
Payments received on account	114	110	114	110
Trade creditors	31,988	26,174	29,606	24,438
Fixed asset creditors	1,076	745	1,076	745
Corporation tax	8,418	5,565	8,008	5,162
Other taxes and social security	686	2,343	686	2,347
Proposed dividend	927	762	927	762
	53,002	44,545	49,244	41,442

16 Creditors—amounts falling due after more than one year

	Group 1986	Group 1985	Holding company 1986	Holding company 1985
Amounts owed to subsidiary companies	—	—	2,752	670
Loan (secured)	200	200	200	200
	200	200	2,952	870

The loan of £200,000 is secured by a charge on one of the freehold properties. It is repayable in 1995 with a premium of £30,000. Interest is payable at $10\frac{3}{4}$% per annum.